Olympic
Marathon

Delfo Cabrera passes an ailing Etienne Gailly on the track to win the 1948 marathon. Used by permission of the International Olympic Committee.

OLYMPIC MARATHON

A Centennial History of the Games' Most Storied Race

Charlie Lovett

 PRAEGER

Westport, Connecticut
London

Library of Congress Cataloging-in-Publication Data

Lovett, Charles C.
    Olympic marathon : a centennial history of the games' most storied
race / Charlie Lovett.
      p.   cm.
    Includes bibliographical references and index.
    ISBN 0–275–95771–3 (alk. paper)
    1. Marathon running—History. 2. Olympics—History. I. Title.
GV1065.L69   1997
796.42'52—dc21   96–47618

British Library Cataloguing in Publication Data is available.

Library of Congress Catalog Card Number: 96–47618
ISBN: 0–275–95771–3

First published in 1997

Praeger Publishers, 88 Post Road West, Westport, CT 06881
An imprint of Greenwood Publishing Group, Inc.

Printed in the United States of America

The paper used in this book complies with the
Permanent Paper Standard issued by the National
Information Standards Organization (Z39.48–1984).

10 9 8 7 6 5 4 3 2 1

For
Bill Carr
Who Started it All

Contents

Prologue: The Legend

The Modern Olympic Games are perhaps the *most* modern spectacle on the planet. Their pageantry, ritual, and tradition are beamed to billions via satellite, and every facet of their competition is not merely tinged with but ruled by modern technology. Yet the Olympics have their roots in a festival more ancient than the rites of Christianity, Islam, or Buddhism. Indeed if, as has often been suggested, the coliseums and stadiums our society has constructed in the twentieth century will ultimately be viewed as the cathedrals of our time, then the Olympic Games are our most sacred rite and Olympic champions our high priests. But the Olympics began in a time before satellites and television, a time before electronic timers, photo finishes, and computer rankings, a time when the greatest of gods was not sport, but Zeus.

The origin of the ancient Olympic Games is shrouded in legend, but it may have begun as a commemoration of Zeus' defeating Kronos in a wrestling match—the prize being possession of the earth. The exact date of the first Olympic Games is also lost. Some sources say 1253 B.C., others 884 B.C.. One thing is certain, however, every four years from 776 B.C. until 394 A.D., the strongest and swiftest men in Greece assembled to compete in the Olympic Games.

The Games were held in Olympia, a great complex that included a 60,000-seat stadium, a vast hippodrome for equestrian events, and a gymnasium for wrestlers, boxers, gymnasts, and others. Religious buildings were also an important part of Olympia, just as religious ceremonies were an important part of the Games. One building, the Olympium, housed a forty-foot ivory statue of Zeus with robes of gold, one of the seven wonders of the world.

With Zeus watching over the Olympics the Games grew in both size and importance. Wars were suspended during the time of Olympic competition, so great was the respect given the Games. The Olympics began with a single footrace, but grew to encompass a variety of events, many similar to those in modern track and field. However, no race in the ancient Olympics was greater than twenty-four laps around the Olympic stadium, a distance of about three miles.

The ancient Greeks were no strangers to long-distance running, but to them it served as a means to communicate not to compete. The Greeks used foot couriers to take important messages from city to city. Out of this tradition grew a legend so persistent that it would spark the imagination of men nearly 2,500 years later.

In 490 B.C. an army from Persia landed on the plain of Marathon, about twenty-five miles from Athens, with the intention of capturing and enslaving that city. The Athenians prepared for a battle that would determine the course of history for centuries to come. A victory for the powerful Persian Empire could destroy the independence of the Greek city-states and effectively end Greek civilization and culture.

While the massive Persian army landed, the Athenians sent a messenger named Philippides (his name was corrupted in later texts to Pheidippides) to Sparta to enlist the aid of the Spartans in the upcoming battle. He covered the distance of about 150 miles in less than two days, a remarkable accomplishment by any standard.

Back at Marathon, however, the decision was made not to wait for the Spartans. The Athenian army fell upon the vastly larger Persian forces while they were still preparing for battle. Against great odds, the Greeks prevailed. Though historians writing close to the time of the battle make no mention of the event, writers some 600 years later claim that a runner was dispatched to Athens to carry the news of the great victory. According to legend he reached the city, said, "Rejoice, we conquer," and fell to the ground dead. Though one source gives the runner's name as Philippides, it is highly unlikely that he would have made such a run after having just run to Sparta. If he had, contemporary historians would surely have noted it.

Whether any messenger at all was sent to Athens with the news of victory is a matter of some doubt, but certainly Philippides was not the messenger. Still, in the centuries that followed, the legend of Pheidippides (as he began to be called) and the legend of a runner who died to bring news of victory to the Athenians merged, and many later writers gave the name Pheidippides to the ill-fated runner. In the nineteenth century Robert Browning wrote in his *Dramatic Idylls* of Pheidippides' dash to Athens, his announcement of victory, and his death. Though Pheidippides was certainly not the runner who carried the news of Greek victory to Athens, and though it seems unlikely that any professional foot courier of ancient Greece would have perished after such a run, the legend took hold, and out of that legend grew the modern marathon race.

In 394 A.D., the Roman Emperor Theodosius banned all non-Christian celebrations in the Empire, effectively putting an end to the Olympic Games. Religion, for the time being, had separated from and usurped sport.

In the mid-1900s, interest in ancient Greece was on the rise. Archaeologists began to uncover the ruins of the ancient stadium at Olympia, and the idea of reviving the Olympic Games was pursued by a Greek businessman named Evangelios Zappas. With the support of the Greek government, Zappas staged an Olympic competition on November 15, 1859. That competition and three others (in 1870, 1875, and 1889) staged by the Greek government with money left by Zappas in his will, were not successful. Because of poor planning and improper facilities, spectators could not see the competition and some got into fights, which spilled over onto the track. It appeared that the Olympic Games, dormant for 1,500 years, would not continue into the new century.

A French baron named Pierre de Coubertin changed all that. Coubertin was an aristocrat who had worked for some years to improve the quality of physical education in France. In addition to a keen interest in athletics, Coubertin was a proponent of internationalism—cooperation between nations which he felt would promote peace. Inspired by the uncovering of the ruins at Olympia, the failed efforts to revive the ancient Games, and his interest in sports, Coubertin conceived the idea of reestablishing the Olympic Games. In 1892, he hosted a banquet for the Union of French Athletic Sports Clubs, a group he had founded five years earlier. In a speech at the banquet, he proposed reviving the Olympic Games, but the suggestion was met with a mixture of apathy and derision. Was Coubertin suggesting holding footraces in the nude as the ancient Greeks had? Was he seriously suggesting that civilized Europeans should compete with Africans and Asians?

Despite the close-mindedness of his compatriots, Coubertin did not give up. In 1894 he hosted an International Congress of Amateurs. On the program, after several topics concerning amateurism and sports, he listed "Reestablishment of the Olympic Games." The congress was not to discuss whether to revive the Olympics, but rather how it should be done. By the end of the conference, Coubertin had formed the International Olympic Committee (IOC), and plans were in place to stage the first modern Olympic Games in Athens, Greece in 1896. He was able to convince delegates from many countries to enthusiastically support the idea. Though much work remained to be done before the Games could begin, Coubertin's dream seemed destined for reality.

Another French delegate to the conference, Michel Bréal, a linguist and historian, was enthralled by the legend of Pheidippides and the famous run from Marathon to Athens. Though the run was unrelated to Olympic competition, Bréal proposed the establishment of a long-distance footrace to commemorate the effort. He offered a silver trophy to whomever would win such a race. Coubertin loved the idea and promoted the race in many speeches he gave to stir up interest in the Games. The new race was called "the marathon" and was included as the final event on the Olympic agenda.

Thus, out of an accomplishment by an ancient Greek, a legend corrupted by historians and poets from Greece to England, and the dreams of two Frenchmen, was born the most audacious of races, the marathon. Little did Bréal know that he had struck a chord that would resonate ever louder as the next century progressed. For there is something in man that seeks out challenge, especially the challenge of a single man taking on a task in which all the forces of nature, and often the opinions of men, are arrayed against him; a task in which his own solitude may become his greatest enemy; a task that his own drive, his own desire, and his own ego cannot fail to make him accomplish. There is something in man that makes him climb mountains because they are there, that makes him explore space because no one has gone there before. There is something in man that seeks out the challenge of the unknown. As the world around us became more and more known in this century, man increasingly turned to the unknown within himself and sought to challenge the limits of his very being. There is something in man that makes him run marathons.

There is, too, something in the Olympic Games that makes its marathon the greatest of all, not merely because it was first or because the legend of Pheidippides links the race to ancient Greece. After the first modern Olympic Games in Athens in 1896, a group from Boston that had competed for the United States returned home full of excitement about the marathon race they had witnessed. The result of that excitement was the establishment of the Boston Marathon the following year.

Run every April since 1897, the Boston race is considered by some the most prestigious of all marathons. After all, the Olympic race is run only every four years, while Boston is an annual race. How many great marathoners will be denied an Olympic medal because they are not at the peak of their career in the right year? Boston is run in the cool weather of New England spring, while the Olympic race is run in the often unfavorably hot conditions of midsummer. How can such poor running conditions produce a true champion?

Yet winning the Olympic Marathon remains the ultimate accomplishment for a long-distance runner, in part because of the very limitations of the race. Like any other long-distance race, the Olympic Marathon requires strength, courage, and endurance but it also requires something else, something the skeptics might call luck but which those versed in their Olympic history might call the blessing of the gods. So, if many of the world's greatest marathoners were never Olympic champions, it is all the more reason to praise the few who have triumphed in this race, for in the religion that twentieth-century sport has become, they have truly been touched by the gods.

Part I

The Men's Race

I

The Games of the I Olympiad: Athens, 1896

As the Athens Olympics approached, the marathon race was viewed with interest, excitement, and concern. Individual feats of long-distance running had been recorded in years past. In the 1700s Foster Powell ran all over England, covering a 402-mile round-trip at age sixty. From 1870–1890, six-day races became popular in England and the United States. Some runners covered over 600 miles during these races, but most of the contests were held on tracks with runners taking rests. The notion of a footrace on the hot and dusty country roads of Greece contested by an international group of amateur competitors and covering a distance of nearly twenty-five miles was unprecedented. Some medical experts warned that such a race would be extremely dangerous to the runners.

When Michel Bréal and Pierre de Coubertin had proposed the idea of the marathon race to the Athens Olympic Organizing Committee, the Greeks had embraced the plan with enthusiasm. Here, after all, was a race that grew out of Greek history and commemorated the feat of a Greek runner. Georgious Averoff, a Greek businessman who was the primary financial backer of the Athens Olympics and who had designed and paid for the restoration of the ancient Panathenaic Stadium in which many of the events would take place, was a supporter of the race, as was Ionnis Lambros, a wealthy collector of Greek antiquities. Lambros offered an antique vase to be added to Bréal's cup as the prize for the marathon champion.

Eager to excel in the marathon competition, the Greeks held a race over the proposed Olympic course to select their team. According to some sources as many as three Greek men died while training for the marathon, so choosing a well-conditioned team was important. The Olympic trial, held on March 10, 1896, was the first organized marathon race ever run, but two runners had run the course in February. Then, only G. Grigorou covered the entire course on foot—his time was three hours and forty-five minutes (3:45). Twelve runners, all members of Greek sports clubs, entered the trial race. The winner was Charilaos Vasilakos, who completed the course in 3:18. Spiridon Belokas and Demetrios Deliyannis rounded out the top three spots. Only a few days before the Games were set to begin, the Greek officials, eager to field the best team possible, held a second trial. This race was won by Mr. Lavrentis, whose first name was not recorded, in 3:11:27, an improvement of nearly seven minutes over the winning time in the first trial. Although entries into the Games were officially closed, additional names were added to the team, including the name of Spiridon Louis, who had finished fifth in the trial.

On the afternoon of Friday, April 10, seventeen runners gathered on the Marathon bridge to await the start of the first Olympic Marathon. Among the competitors were the Australian Edwin Flack, who had already won gold medals in the 800 and 1,500 meter races. Flack lived in London, where he worked as an accountant, but he held the Australian national record for the mile. Arthur Blake of the United States, the second place finisher in the 1,500 meters was another threat along with Albin Lermusiaux of France, third in the 1,500 meters, and Gyula Kellner of Hungary. The rest of the field was made up entirely of Greeks who had had some experience on the course from running the trial races. The race would cover a distance of forty kilometers (24.8 miles). Of the non-Greek competitors, only Kellner had ever run such a distance.

One foreigner had been disqualified before the start of the race. Carlo Airoldi had traveled nearly a thousand miles from his home in Italy to Athens on foot, only to be kept out of the race on the grounds that he was a professional athlete. Airoldi had more experience at long-distance racing than any of the entrants in the Olympic race, having run several fifty kilometer races. But the Olympics, as Coubertin had planned, adhered to a strict code of amateurism. The Italian would not race.

In the earlier track and field events, the Americans had been dominant, and the Greeks were desperate for a victory. The marathon was considered the highlight of the Games. A failure by the Greeks to win the event would mean deep disappointment and resentment. Even the foreigners in the crowd of over 100,000 that lined the road and filled the stadium where the race would finish hoped for a Greek victory.

The race began just before 2:00 P.M. The competitors had traveled to Marathon the night before in wagons. They had drawn lots to determine their starting position and now a small crowd of villagers watched as Major Papadimantopoulos gave a short speech and then fired his pistol into the air to begin the first Olympic Marathon.

The runners were escorted not by motorcycles and television trucks as in today's marathons, but by officials and doctors on bicycles and in horse-drawn wagons. The Frenchman Lermusiaux took the early lead, setting a fast pace even by modern standards. He reached the village of Pikermi, more than halfway into the race, in a mere fifty-five minutes, leading by nearly two miles over the Australian Flack, the American Blake, and the Hungarian Kellner. No Greeks were running in the top four spots, and Spiridon Louis was well back in the pack. Some time later, when Louis reached Pikermi, he enjoyed a glass of wine and expressed his certainty that he would win the race.

After Pikermi, the road turned uphill and the leaders began to regret the early pace. Blake dropped out less than a mile after the village, Kellner slowed and was overtaken by the Greek Vasilakos, winner of the first trial race. Lermusiaux began to drop his pace, but he still led at the village of Karavati, where the peasants crowned him with a victor's floral wreath. Shortly past the village, Lermusiaux weakened further. When a fellow Frenchman bumped him with a bicycle, he fell and was passed by Flack. Though he rose to his feet, he could not run much further, and near the twenty-mile mark he collapsed and was carried away.

With six miles to go, Flack led the race and he sent a bicyclist off to the stadium to announce his impending victory. This news sent the crowd gathered in the stadium into a sad silence. Meanwhile, behind Flack, Spiridon Louis had passed the Hungarian Kellner, as well as several Greek runners, to move into second place. Flack was exhausted, and less than a mile later, Louis passed him and pulled into a lead of about twenty yards. For two and a half miles they ran in sight of each other, until Louis finally put on a burst of speed and Flack, unable to catch him, staggered and fell and was carried from the course. During this battle for the lead, Greek runners had moved into second and third place.

Again a messenger left the race to bring news to the stadium, but this time the news was joyful. The starter of the race rode on horseback into the stadium and rushed to the royal box to deliver the message to the king. In an instant the news spread and the stadium erupted in shouts of celebration. A Greek would win the marathon!

Louis ran through the streets of Athens, barely able to pass through the joyous throng that greeted him. When he entered the stadium, he was joined by the Crown Prince Nicholas and Prince George who ran with him to the finish line and then carried him in triumph to the royal box. Louis was an instant national hero, and his victory erased all hard feelings about the earlier triumphs of the Americans and other foreigners. He had completed the race in a time of 2:58:50, a remarkable improvement over the times posted by the winners of the trial races.

Second across the line, over seven minutes later, was Charilaos Vasilakos, winner of the first Greek trial race, who was followed in short order by another Greek, Spiridon Belokas, and then the Hungarian Kellner. The crowd was in ecstasy seeing their countrymen sweep the top three spots. Kellner later complained, however, that Belokas had covered part of the course not on foot but in a carriage. Belokas promptly admitted his guilt and third place was awarded to the Hungarian. It was not the last time that the marathon finish would be tinged with controversy.

The Greeks were not bothered with such trifles, however. Louis' victory had provided just the emotional boost that was necessary to keep the Olympic movement alive. Had an American or Frenchman won the coveted marathon, the disappointment of the crowd might have doomed the Olympic movement. As it was, the hysterical celebration of Greeks and visitors alike propelled the modern Olympic movement into the twentieth century.

The marathon was the final competition of the Olympics, but two more events remained before the Games would be over—the King's breakfast and the award ceremony. On Sunday, two days after the marathon, King George held an elegant breakfast at which the athletes were honored guests. Spiridon Louis attracted as much attention as anyone, not only because of the excitement generated by his victory, but also because he came to the breakfast dressed in the national uniform of Greece—a narrow jacket, flared fustanella (something like a short skirt), tights, and boots. Following the breakfast, Louis was met by his adoring father and the two drove through the streets of Athens, the father revelling in the glory of the son.

The following Wednesday, the stadium was packed to watch the awards ceremony. The winner of each event was awarded an olive branch and a silver medal (there were no gold medals in the first modern Olympics). A laurel branch and a bronze medal commemorated second place. For a few events, special cups had been given as well. The last to receive his award was Louis, whose appearance on the platform was the cause of huge celebration in the stands. In addition to his olive branch and medal, he received the silver cup that Michel Bréal, who had conceived the marathon race, had donated. Louis also was presented with the antique vase given by Ionnis Lambros. On the vase was painted a contestant in a footrace at the ancient Olympic Games. Louis later donated the vase to a museum.

Despite offers of money, goods, services, and even a hand in marriage, Louis returned to his village, accepting, as one story would have it, only the offer of a horse and cart that the villagers needed to haul water. Many myths and legends grew up around Louis following his famous victory—so many that it is difficult to ascertain the truth about him. He was twenty-four years old and from the village of Maroussi and, according to which source you believe, he was a poor shepherd, a well-off farmer, a postal messenger, a soldier, or a peasant. His story even inspired a novelization, and the expression *"egine Louis,"* which can be translated as "to become like Louis" or "take off like Louis," has became part of the Greek language.

Spiridon Louis, and all who had taken part in the first Olympic Marathon, had foreshadowed the creed that Pierre de Coubertin, inspired by a sermon at St. Paul's Cathedral on the eve of the 1908 Games, would write for the Olympics: "The most important thing in the Olympic Games is not to win but to take part, just as the most important thing in life is not the triumph but the struggle. The essential thing is not to have conquered but to have fought well." In no Olympic event is the importance of those words more evident than in the marathon, and in the next century of Olympic marathons, competitors would consider taking part and fighting well the greatest victories of all.

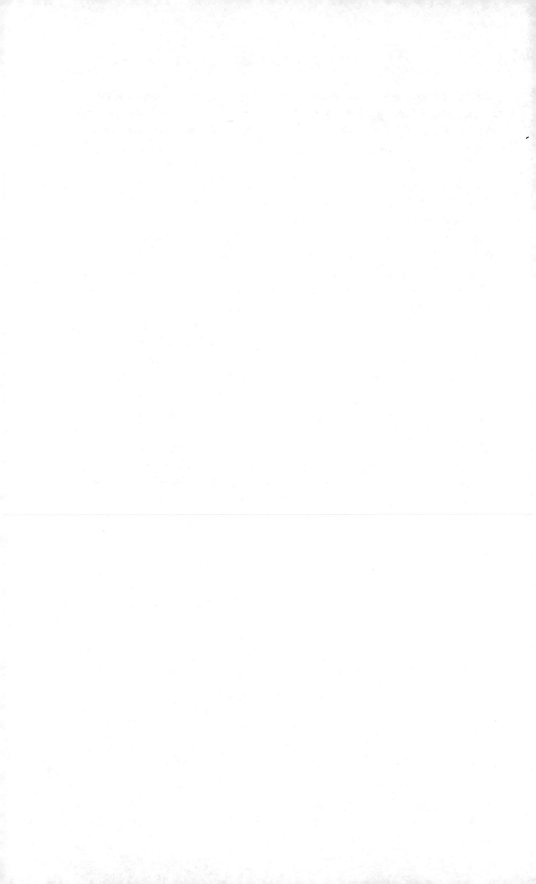

2

The Games of the II Olympiad: Paris, 1900

If the victory by Spiridon Louis assured the future of the Olympics by rousing the spirits of the Greek and foreign spectators at the Athens Games, the next two Olympiads nearly succeeded in burying the movement. The Games of 1900 and 1904 were held in Paris and St. Louis respectively and in both cases they were held in conjunction with International Expositions. The events were spread out over a period of several months in both cities with little press coverage and few spectators. Many of the competitors did not even know they were competing in the Olympics. Michel Théato, the winner of the Paris marathon, received a medal in the mail twelve years later and discovered that he had won the Olympic Marathon.

By bringing the 1900 Olympic Games to Paris, Baron Pierre de Coubertin hoped to merge the country of his birth with the competition of his dreams. He envisioned a grand Olympic complex, modeled on the Greek stadium, where all the events would be held. The organizers of the Universal Exposition, however, quickly squelched Coubertin's vision, and put Daniel Merillon in charge of planning the "International Championships." From beginning to end the five-month Paris Games were poorly organized, and no race demonstrated that better than the marathon.

The marathon course began with four laps on the track of the Racing Club de France, then passed through the Bois de Boulogne, and wound through the narrow streets of Paris, near old city walls and through slums, before returning to the starting point. Despite its convoluted path, the course was poorly marked and only a few officials were posted along the way to keep runners headed in the right direction. To add to this confusion, the race was scheduled on July 19, a day when the temperature hit 102°F. Not surprisingly, only eight of the nineteen starters were able to finish. The one positive note in the statistics of the race was the number of countries represented—up to seven from five. The marathon was becoming more international.

The race itself was as confusing as the course. American Arthur Newton moved into first place at about the halfway mark, or so he thought. Convinced that he had lead the entire second half of the race, he crossed the finish line to discover that he was fifth. The winner, Michel Théato, had finished over an hour earlier. Newton and his American teammates accused Théato, a twenty-three-year-old bread deliveryman, of cheating, claiming that he had taken short cuts through the streets of Paris he knew so well. The second and fourth place finishers were also Frenchmen, Emile Champion and Eugene Resse, and Newton insisted that he had been robbed. However, the third place finisher, Ernst Fast, was from Sweden and had little knowledge of Paris streets. In fact, Fast had become lost on the course and when he asked a policeman for directions, the gendarme pointed him in the wrong direction. Like so much else in this race, that incident caused controversy—but in this case, legend has it that the police officer became so depressed over his mistake that he later shot himself.

The main argument against Newton's claim of victory was the finishing times. Théato finished in 2:59:45, almost exactly the same time as Louis' 2:58:50 in 1896 (given the fact that the Paris course was about 275 yards longer). Newton, however, crossed the line in a very uncompetitive time of 4:04:12. In all likelihood, Newton became lost on the confusing course and ran much further than Théato. Whether the winner ran the full distance, as he claimed and as the officials ruled, we will never know.

Another American runner also had cause to complain. Dick Grant unsuccessfully sued the IOC claiming that a bicyclist had knocked him down as he was challenging for the lead in the race.

Théato went on to set a French record in the 10,000 meters, before turning professional in 1902. He ran a race of just under twenty-five miles later that year, but placed only ninth.

The combination of a poorly marked course and little or no marshalling or crowd control made the Paris marathon somewhat embarrassing. The embarrassment was added to by the fact that few present had any idea that the Olympic Marathon was being run. Not until twelve years later were Olympic medals sent to the contenders and Théato's victory officially confirmed. But the most bizarre years of the Olympic Marathon had just begun.

3

The Games of the III Olympiad:
St. Louis, 1904

The 1904 Olympic Games had originally been slated for Chicago, but when the organizers of the World's Fair and Louisiana Purchase Exposition in St. Louis announced their plans to hold an international athletic competition in the same year, Chicago organizers agreed to let St. Louis have the Olympics rather than hold competing meets.

As in Paris, the Games were spread out over several months, but the Americans made them a featured event of the Fair, not the mere side show they had been in Paris. Three hundred and nine events were held between July and November, though only eighty-eight would be recognized by the IOC. Unfortunately, the Games were only slightly more international than an American championship. Of the 617 athletes who participated, 525 were American and 41 were Canadian. The other fifty-one represented ten additional countries. Europe, home of many record holders and world-class athletes, was not well represented. The British and others were distracted by the Russo-Japanese War, and the French, it is said, were stinging over their foolish sale of the Louisiana Territory, the centenary of which was being celebrated at the St. Louis Exposition. Even Pierre de Coubertin stayed at home.

In the midst of these heavily American Games, on August 30, thirty-two runners from five nations lined up to compete in the most difficult Olympic Marathon in history. To begin with, the organizers knew virtually nothing about staging a marathon. The race was scheduled to be run in the middle of the afternoon on a day when the temperature would hover around 90°F. After five laps around the stadium track, the course passed over seven steep hills on extremely dusty country roads before returning to the stadium. The dusty conditions were made far worse by the vehicles that preceded and followed the runners. Technology began to intrude on the race, with steam-powered automobiles carrying race officials, medical personnel, and each runner's attendants. Finally, the only refreshment made available to the runners was water from a well at about the twelve-mile mark. Though any marathoner prepares for a gruelling race before he toes the starting line, no one had prepared for the unforgiving and unforgivable conditions they would face in St. Louis.

Even the start was bizarre. One of the runners stood at the line wearing heavy street shoes, long work pants, and a long sleeved shirt. His name was Felix Carvajal, and he had come all the way from Havana, Cuba to run the race. Carvajal had raised the money for his trip by giving running exhibitions in Havana, but he lost his money in a crap game after his steamer arrived in New Orleans. Undaunted, he hitchhiked to St. Louis and arrived at the start of the marathon in his street clothes. The start of the race was delayed while American Martin Sheridan, who would win the gold medal in the discus a few days later, found a pair of scissors and cut off Carvajal's trousers above the knee.

Carvajal seemed as unfazed by the heat and the dust as he did by his inappropriate attire. He stopped several times along the course, chatting with spectators and practicing his English. To combat thirst, he took some peaches from an official in one of the cars and at one point left the course to pick green apples in an orchard. Despite stomach cramps brought on by this last antic, Carvajal finished fourth, a remarkable achievement under the circumstances.

Among the other starters were Lentauw and Yamasani, two Kaffir tribesmen from Zululand, South Africa, who became the first two black Africans to compete in the Olympic Games. They had been in St. Louis as part of the Boer War exhibit at the World's Fair and decided to enter the marathon. Despite being run off the road and chased through a corn field by two large dogs, Lentauw finished in ninth place, and his countryman finished twelfth. The Americans fielded a number of hopefuls, including Arthur Newton, out to redeem himself after Paris, and the winners of the past three Boston Marathons. Thomas Hicks and Fred Lorz of the United States had finished second and fifth respectively in the most recent Boston race and were considered in peak shape. Frenchman Albert Corey had run poorly in the Paris marathon in 1900 and hoped to prove his worth in St. Louis. He had been working as a strikebreaker in Chicago since 1903, so he was able to travel to St. Louis for the race, in spite of the fact that France sent no official team. To this field were added, among others, ten volunteer Greeks who, though not a part of an official Greek team, hoped to bring honor to their country by repeating the feat of Spiridon Louis.

The race for gold in this marathon was as much a race against the conditions as against the other contestants. Fred Lorz took the early lead and was soon joined by four other runners. Soon the pack began to spread out and Sam Mellor, winner of the 1902 Boston Marathon, moved into the lead. At nine miles Lorz dropped out. Shortly after that, Mellor looked as if he might drop out as well. Slowing to a walk he was passed by Arthur Newton. Mellor put on one more burst to regain the lead before finally dropping out after the fifteen-mile mark.

Mellor's demise left English-born Thomas Hicks of Cambridge, Massachusetts, in the lead. But Hicks, who had run well through the first half of the race, also began to show signs of exhaustion. Throughout the latter stages of the race he was given help by his handlers, Charles Lucas and Hugh McGrath. With less than ten miles to go, Hicks, with a lead of a mile and a half, asked to lie down. Instead, his handlers gave him a dose of strychnine mixed with a raw egg white. Three miles later he was given another dose of strychnine, more eggs, and some French brandy. His handlers also used water warmed on the engine of one of the automobiles to bathe him.

Lucas later described Hicks's condition in the final stages of the race: "His eyes were dull, lusterless; the ashen color of his skin and face had deepened; his arms appeared as weights well tied down; he could scarcely lift his legs which his knees were almost stiff." Suffering from what Lucas called hallucination, Hicks seemed to think he was still twenty miles from the finish. "His mind continually roved toward something to eat," wrote Lucas, "and in the last mile Hicks continually harped on the subject."[1]

With Hicks in such condition, it was not surprising to see him passed by another runner, but the runner looked much too fresh to have run the gruelling course. In fact, it was Fred Lorz, who had dropped out earlier and taken a ride part of the way, who now passed Hicks heading back to the stadium.

Hicks slowed to a walk when he reached the final hill two miles from the finish. More strychnine and brandy (borrowed from another trainer, as Hicks's personal supply had run out) revived him again and Hicks entered the stadium, shuffling around the track to finish in a time of 3:28. Photographs of Hicks in the final stages of the race clearly show that he was physically assisted, being held up by two men running at his side. A protest was later filed against Hicks, not because he had received assistance, but because he had been paced by an automobile. This protest was overruled by officials. In spite of the assistance and the drugs, both of which would be grounds for disqualification in later Olympiads, Hicks was awarded the gold medal and a special silver cup.

But even the finish of the race was not without confusion. Some fifteen minutes before Hicks crossed the line, Fred Lorz had entered the stadium, looking remarkably well for someone who had just negotiated the arduous marathon course. Lorz was cheered by the crowd and the President's daughter, Alice Roosevelt, insisted on having her picture taken with the champion. Lorz said nothing about the fact that he had ridden part of the way in a truck. He was about to be awarded the gold medal when Hicks entered the stadium and the officials who accompanied him cried foul.

Lorz immediately admitted to his crime, explaining that the truck he had ridden in had broken down four miles from the stadium and he had run the rest of the way. He insisted that he was only playing a practical joke and that he had every intention of confessing, but the officials were not amused. Lorz was banned from running competitions for life by the Amateur Athletic Union (AAU) of the United States, the organization that certified track and field competitions. The ban was subsequently lifted, however, and Lorz went on to win the 1905 Boston Marathon.

Once Hicks was revealed as the real winner, the attention of the crowd, and of Alice Roosevelt, turned to him. Hicks, however, was in no condition to revel in his victory. The combination of the drugs and the exhaustion had left him in a stupor. Not until he had eaten a large dinner did he recover enough to receive the Francis Trophy presented to the marathon winner. He told the crowd at the award ceremony that he would rather have won the marathon than be elected president.

Following Hicks into the stadium was Albert Corey, the Frenchman who had been so disappointed in his finish in Paris in 1900. Corey crossed the finish line in 3:34:52, six minutes after Hicks. In third place, some thirteen minutes after Corey, was the American Arthur Newton who had thought he won gold in Paris. Though he did not win the race, he did redeem his Paris performance with a bronze medal.

Hicks, Corey, and Newton, along with two Africans and an intrepid Cuban had triumphed over the horrendous conditions, but others were not so lucky. Only fourteen of the thirty-two starters finished the race. John Lordon, winner of the 1903 Boston Marathon, began vomiting at the ten-mile mark and dropped out. William Garcia, a runner from San Francisco, suffered worst of all. Garcia collapsed midway through the race and was found lying in the middle of the road, apparently near death. He was taken to the hospital where doctors discovered that large amounts of dust had nearly destroyed his stomach lining. Had he arrived at the hospital even an hour later, he would certainly have died.

Like Garcia, the Olympic movement suffered greatly at the hands of the St. Louis organizers, as it had in Paris. Combining the Olympic Games with a World's Fair robbed the Games of the attention they deserved. Though the marathon had not seen its last controversial ending, it had, in Paris and St. Louis, seen its lowest point and its slowest winning times. Like the Olympics themselves, though, the marathon would recover and go on to glory. And, like the Olympics, what the race needed was another shot of Greece.

4

The Intercalated Games:
Athens, 1906

At the 1896 Olympic Games, King George of Greece had suggested that his country serve as the permanent host of the Games. Coubertin tactfully pretended not to understand the suggestion, but shortly thereafter he mollified the Greeks by suggesting that Athens host an interim games two years after each Olympiad. The Athens Games of 1906 were the only such "Intercalated Games" ever held, partly because of later political unrest in Greece, but they were important in rescuing the Olympics from the sideshow they had become in 1900 and 1904.

As in 1896, the Games were once again an event in their own right, and spectators played a central role in their success. For the first time many national teams, including the team from the United States, received official sanction from their countries. Previous Olympic Games had featured fractured American teams composed of individual groups from colleges and athletic clubs. The 1906 U.S. team was chosen by an American Olympic Committee, with President Teddy Roosevelt serving as honorary chairman. The team's trip to Greece was financed by a nationwide fund drive, making this the first real U.S. Olympic team.

Twenty nations were represented by 884 athletes at the 1906 Games, and this expansion in the field of athletes was reflected in the makeup of the marathon race, which featured fifty-three runners from fifteen nations. Once again, the marathon race captured the imagination of the Greeks; all of Athens longed for a Greek victor. This time, the offers to any Greek who might win the race included a loaf of bread and three cups of coffee every day for a year, free shaves for life, a year's worth of Sunday luncheons, and a statue of Hermes.

Billy Sherring, a railway brakeman from Hamilton, Ontario, Canada, believed that the merchants were safe in making these offers. He believed that not a Greek, but a Canadian would win the race, and that Canadian would be Billy Sherring.

He had saved as much as he could to pay his passage to Greece, and a local athletic club had chipped in $75, but Sherring still could not scrape together the money he needed for the trip. Finally, he took his $75 to a bartender who bet it on a horse named Cicely. Cicely won, paid 6–1 odds, and Billy Sherring was on his way to Greece.

Sherring arrived in Greece two months before the Games, working as a railway porter to pay his expenses and training every other day. On March 17, a trial run was held by the Greeks and the winner finished in a time of 3:04:29. Unknown to the competitors, Sherring had secretly covered the same course twenty minutes faster. Acclimatized to the 80°F weather and sure of his ability on the course, Sherring felt confident that he would strike gold on May 1, the day of the marathon.

Perhaps because of the interference of Thomas Hicks's attendants in the 1904 marathon, the Greek organizing committee had drawn up rules governing the assistance that runners could receive. Each runner was allowed to be followed by a single bicycle-riding attendant. The attendant could provide medicine or refreshment during the race, but if the runner was aided at any time by two or more attendants, he would be disqualified.

The Greeks also took care to plan a safer race than the one run in St. Louis. Every five kilometers were manned checkpoints with refreshments and medical personnel. Organizers were starting to learn how a marathon race should be run.

As they had in 1896, the runners left from the village of Marathon, where they had travelled the night before by carriage. The starter's gun was fired at 3:00 P.M. George Blake of Australia was the early leader in the race, staging a duel with American William Frank. Frank took the lead after four miles, but three miles later he was again passed by Blake. Blake began to slow, however, and was passed by Frank at the fifteen-mile mark. By this time, Frank had been joined by Sherring, and the two men ran together for three more miles.

Eighteen miles into the race, Sherring turned to Frank, said, "Well, good-bye, Billy," and surged ahead, building up a large enough lead that he walked part of the way and still won by nearly seven minutes, in a time of

2:51:23. Although the course had been slightly longer than any previous Olympic Marathon, and over a mile longer than the 1896 route, Sherring had bettered the previous best time of Spiridon Louis by over seven minutes. Frank finished in third place with a time of 3:00:46, having been passed by John Svanberg of Sweden who took second in 2:58:23.

The crowd in the Olympic stadium was disappointed when news arrived that no Greek was in contention for the lead, but the good-natured Greeks honored Sherring when he entered the stadium. Prince George met him at the entrance to the stadium and ran around the track with him to the finish where Sherring, like Spiridon Louis ten years before, bowed to the king. Queen Olga sent a large bouquet of flowers to the victorious Sherring on the track. Although he did not receive all of the gifts that had been offered to a Greek winner, Sherring was given a three-foot statue of Athena and a lamb.

This latter prize might have been inspired by Sherring's apparent need for fattening up. He had weighed 135 pounds on arrival in Greece and had trimmed down to 112 by the start of the race. By the race's end, his reported weight was ninety-eight pounds. Sherring returned to Canada, where his hometown gave him a prize of several thousand dollars, which was augmented by a few hundred more from the city of Toronto.

Though the marathon of 1906 was not an official Olympic event, it produced better times and less controversy than any of the previous Olympic races. It was also the unofficial Olympic debut of an Italian runner named Dorando Pietri, who had dropped out of the race after about thirteen miles, complaining of stomach cramps. Pietri, then twenty years old, had won the Italian Olympic trial on a course of about twenty-five miles, in a time of 2:42. In Athens he made little impact on the world, but two years later, in the Games of the IV Olympiad in London, he would provide the most dramatic moment in Olympic Marathon history.

5

The Games of the IV Olympiad: London, 1908

The 1908 Olympic Games had originally been awarded to Rome, but the Italians had difficulty in preparing for the event, so it was decided to move the Games to London. The British Olympic Organizing Committee, under the leadership of Lord Desborough, made splendid preparations, constructing a stadium with a capacity of nearly 70,000. From the opening of the Games, however, there was antagonism between the British and the Americans—antagonism that would carry on to the track at the finish of the marathon.

To begin with, the British had failed to fly the American flag at the Opening Ceremonies. From then on, a steady stream of American protests of British rules and officiating marred the track-and-field competition. The battle culminated with the final of the 400 meters, which featured an Englishman and three Americans. One of the Americans ran wide on the final stretch to avoid being passed by the British runner. The British officials broke the tape before the race could finish and announced that another final would have to be run. Two days later, with the Americans boycotting the race in protest, Wyndham Halswelle of Great Britain ran the second final all alone to win the gold medal. Years later, those present would claim that neither the British nor the Americans had exhibited fine sportsmanship. In any case, by the start of the marathon, conflicts had been raging for several days.

The British organizers had elected to begin the marathon on the grounds of Windsor Castle, twenty-six miles from White City Stadium, where the race would end. The starting point was chosen so that the children of King

Edward VII and Queen Alexandra could watch and was coordinated with a birthday celebration for one of the children. The course passed through quaint villages and along the banks of the Thames towards White City. In the stadium, the runners would circle 385 yards of the track to end in front of the royal box of Queen Alexandra. This distance of 26 miles and 385 yards would eventually become the standard length for all marathons. In its distance, therefore, the 1908 Olympic Marathon is the first that can be compared to current races.

On July 24, at 2:30 in the afternoon, fifty-six runners from sixteen nations lined up in four rows and prepared to set out on the long road from Windsor to White City. The Princess of Wales gave the signal, and Lord Desborough fired the starting gun, sending the runners down a hill past the castle walls and toward London. The early leaders were from the British team, who were eager to deliver a home team win in the prestigious race. Unfortunately, the fast pace in the hot and muggy weather took its toll. The first few miles featured Ted Jack of Scotland in the lead, closely followed by a cluster of British runners. The pace set by Jack, however, was clearly too fast for the muggy conditions. He soon tired and stopped at an official refreshment stand. Though he continued the race, he never regained the lead.

Fred Lord and Jack Price, also of Great Britain, took his place. Five miles later, Lord dropped back and by the halfway mark, Price led by 200 yards over South African Charles Hefferon. Hefferon moved into the lead after the fourteen-mile mark, and Price soon dropped out. The next runner to challenge for the lead was Tom Longboat of Canada, an Onondaga Indian whose entry had been protested by the American team on the grounds that he was a professional. Longboat was unable to catch Hefferon, though, and eventually dropped out of the race. Though the heat claimed many victims that day, the official Canadian report claimed that Longboat's difficulties were caused by drug use. With eight miles to go the race appeared to be narrowed down to Hefferon and the diminutive Italian Dorando Pietri, who had dropped out of the 1906 race. Pietri had moved gradually up through the pack and was now running in second place.

Pietri, a candy maker from Capri, was born on October 16, 1885 and had competed as a bicyclist in two races before he became a runner. In 1905 he won his first national title in a twenty-five kilometer race. He had dropped out of the Italian Marathon Championships in its first year in 1907, and made the Olympic team by setting a record in a forty kilometer track race just seventeen days before the London marathon.

Hefferon led the London marathon by nearly four minutes at the twenty-mile mark, but then Pietri, who raced in a white shirt and red knickerbockers, began to reel him in. In the final miles of the race, both Hefferon and Pietri made crucial mistakes. With Pietri closing the gap, Hefferon accepted a drink of champagne from a spectator. Less than a mile later, he was suffering from stomach cramps and dizziness. For his part, Pietri, encouraged by the cheering crowds that lined the streets, picked up his pace too much and too soon, running the risk that he would exhaust himself. Further ahead, the crowd was now slapping Hefferon on the back over and over in an effort to encourage him. Unfortunately, this show of good will only served to further exhaust the spent runner. A half mile from the stadium, Pietri passed Hefferon and moved into the lead.

Behind the dramatic battle that was unfolding in the lead, the American team of John Hayes, Joseph Forshaw, and Alton Welton, were running strongly and moving up on the weakening leaders. Hayes had finished second in the 1908 Boston Marathon by only twenty seconds and had won the Yonkers Marathon the year before.

Inside the stadium, the crowd waited for the leaders to make their entrance. Word had spread that a South African and an Italian were at the front of the race, and the British crowd hoped that the South African Hefferon, as a member of the British Empire, would bring glory to the homeland. But Dorando Pietri entered the stadium first, and thus began one of the most confusing spectacles in Olympic history.

Pietri was clearly dazed and exhausted when he appeared. At first, he headed the wrong way around the track. Race officials immediately pointed him in the right direction, but within a few yards he collapsed on the track. Olympic crowds love the struggle and triumph of an underdog, and here was a runner they had never heard of collapsing from exhaustion in the final 385 yards of the marathon. The crowd began wildly cheering their support of Pietri. But the officials and doctors were left with the question of what to do. The man clearly needed help, but such help could disqualify him from a race he had nearly won. Feeling they could not leave him prone on the track, race officials helped him back to his feet and he continued on. Pietri rose and fell four times as he moved slowly around the track toward the finish line.

There were some reports that the U.S. delegation had first cried for the officials to help Pietri across the line so the Italian would defeat the representative of the Empire who followed. But all that changed with Pietri still struggling to reach the finish amidst a crowd of doctors and officials, when American John Hayes came on to the track. Hayes had passed Hefferon just outside the stadium and was running strongly in the closing lap of the race. Now the Americans reportedly called for Pietri to be left alone, so that Hayes could pass him and win the race. As Pietri, steps from the finish, began to collapse for the fifth time, Jack Andrew, the organizer of the race, caught the Italian and carried him across the finish line. He later said he was following the instructions of Doctor Bulger, the race's medical officer. The Italian flag was raised on the victory pole as John Hayes crossed the finish followed some twenty-five seconds later by Hefferon.

Of course, the Americans immediately protested that Pietri must be disqualified, because he had received help. Whether the British officials recalled, at the time, the assisted victory of American Thomas Hicks in St. Louis four years earlier, is not known. The assistance given to Pietri was so blatant, however, and had been witnessed by such a crowd, that the officials had no choice but to disqualify him. As Pietri lay recovering on a stretcher, the Italian flag was lowered and replaced by the Stars and Stripes. A little over a minute after Hefferon crossed the line, another American, Joseph Forshaw, finished the race. With Pietri's disqualification, this gave the Americans the gold and bronze medals, equalling their more controversial performance in St. Louis. Never since has the American team had as good a finish in the marathon.

Though Hayes had won the race, Pietri became the hero. Fully recovered the next day he protested that he had not requested assistance and that he could have finished on his own, though this seems highly unlikely given his continual collapsing. The next day arrangements were made for Pietri to receive a special gold cup, a replica of the one awarded to Hayes, from Queen Alexandra, who had witnessed the dramatic finish from her royal box. Sir Arthur Conan Doyle, who may have been one of the doctors on the track at the time of Pietri's collapse, headed up the effort to make this award. On the cup were engraved the words "To Pietri Dorando In Remembrance of the Marathon Race from Windsor to the Stadium July 24, 1908 from Queen Alexandra." When Pietri left London on the train at Charing Cross station, a huge crowd turned out to wish him farewell. In the United States songs were written about Pietri, including one by Irving Berlin.

John Hayes, the official winner of the race, was a twenty-two-year-old clerk at Bloomingdale's in New York. His boss, Mr. Bloomingdale, had taken such a liking to Hayes and his running, that he had constructed a track on the roof of the store for Hayes to train. Bloomingdale gave Hayes vacation with full pay to attend the Olympics and he rewarded the gold medal winner with a promotion to manager of the sporting goods department.

The finish of the marathon had created such a worldwide stir that Pietri and Hayes both soon gave up their jobs to become professional runners. They raced each other twice in New York City in head-to-head marathons, on November 25, 1908 and March 15, 1909, with the Italian winning both contests, one by a mere sixty yards. During this same period, Pietri lost two head-to-head marathons to Tom Longboat, but later took revenge beating Longboat in a twenty kilometer race. Most of the races were run not on the roads but on indoor tracks, where paying spectators could watch the entire contest. In one race, Pietri had to run over 260 laps on a track in Madison Square Garden. Pietri retired in 1911, having won thirty-eight of the fifty-nine amateur races he entered and fifty of his sixty-nine professional races, though of course not all these races were marathons.

His career was impressive, but the world would remember Pietri as the figure who struggled around the track that hot day in London. That event was made all the more famous because it was captured on motion-picture film. Motion pictures made their Olympic debut in 1908.

Pietri's brother ultimately absconded with his earnings, and Dorando returned to Italy and became a taxi driver, also earning money from the government for scouting out promising marathon runners. He died on February 7, 1942.

Historically, the 1908 Olympic Marathon was important for creating the distance that was ultimately adopted as standard for the race. The American marathon craze kicked off by the publicity surrounding Pietri and Hayes helped establish the 1908 distance as standard. But the event will always be remembered for its amazing finish, and for the feat of a courageous Italian determined to see the race through to the end. More than anyone before or after, Pietri served to remind the world that the marathon is, and will always be, the most unpredictable of contests.

6

The Games of the V Olympiad: Stockholm, 1912

The Olympic Games of 1912 were held in Stockholm, appropriate for a Games that featured superb performances by the first of the great Scandinavian distance runners, Finland's Hannes Kolehmainen, who won the 5,000 meters, 10,000 meters, and cross-country races. They were also the Olympics of Jim Thorpe, the Native American who won both the pentathlon and the decathlon.

Sixty-eight runners from nineteen nations started the marathon on July 14, another oppressively hot day for the race. Fully half of the competitors dropped out before the finish because of the heat. Most of the runners wore handkerchiefs or white hats for protection from the brutal Scandinavian sun.

The race included what American organizers felt was the strongest U.S. marathon team ever assembled. Joseph Forshaw of the United States, who had won bronze in London, was joined by Clarence DeMar, whose 2:21:39 in the 1911 Boston Marathon (a race of about twenty-four miles) had improved Tom Longboat's course record by three minutes. Mike Ryan, the captain of the marathon team, had won the 1912 Boston Marathon, setting a new course and American record. Two Native Americans, Andrew Sockalexis and Louis Tewanina, were also on the team. The team totalled twelve runners, the last qualifier being young Gaston Strobino, who had been added when another runner decided not to make the trip.

The American marathon team was coached by John Hayes, the winner of the London race. But marathoners are individuals, and coaching them as a team is not a simple thing. By race day, most of the runners on the team had been offended by the coaches and team officials. They had been forced to change their training schedules to train as a team, and they faced a hot day with little enthusiasm after an unpleasant crossing of the Atlantic and difficult days of training in Europe. Officials had told the team that Ryan, DeMar, or Sockalexis must win the gold, and this proclamation did nothing to remove the tension of the days prior to the race.

Along with the impressive American team, Hannes Kolehmainen's older brother Tatu competed for Finland and Fred Lord, who had led part of the way in London, ran for Great Britain. But none of these impressive runners would win gold that hot day in Stockholm.

The marathon course, which measured about twenty-five miles, began in the Olympic stadium in Stockholm, proceeded into the country to the village of Solentuna, and then returned to finish in the stadium. The roads along the way had been cleared of traffic, swept, and watered, in an effort to keep dust from becoming a problem for the runners. The entire route was lined with spectators, many of whom had arrived early in the morning to obtain a good view of the race. Just before 2:00 P.M. the starter's gun sounded.

A. Ahlgren took the early lead going out of the stadium. At about the three-mile mark, Tatu Kolehmainen, who had dropped out of the 10,000 meters a few days earlier, took over the front spot. Ahlgren followed him closely for several miles, but at about the nine-mile mark, he could take the pace no more and he dropped back leaving Kolehmainen running in front all alone. Thirteen seconds back were South African runners Christian Gitsham and Kenneth McArthur.

Just before the turnaround point, Gitsham moved into a small lead. Then, shortly after the turnaround, American gold medal hopeful Mike Ryan dropped out. Now the front trio consisted of Gitsham, Kolehmainen, and McArthur, followed closely by Fred Lord.

Many of the runners were feeling the effects of the extreme heat, and after fifth place Italian Carlo Speroni asked for a bucket of water to be poured over his head at the halfway mark, many others followed suit.

At the seventeen-mile mark, the two South Africans and the Finn Kolehmainen were running within a few yards of each other, but after another three miles, Kolehmainen could take the pace no longer and dropped out of the race.

Many claimed that the South Africans enjoyed the advantage of having trained in the heat, for they certainly seemed less affected by the conditions than most of the other runners. Clarence DeMar, for instance, slowed to a walk for nearly a mile, one of only two times in a sixty-five–marathon career that he was unable to keep running.

McArthur and Gitsham continued on together until about two miles from the finish, when Gitsham stopped for a drink of water. The two runners had agreed that McArthur would wait while Gitsham got a drink, but he continued on, opening up a lead that was too great to close in the short distance left in the race.

The crowd in the stadium had been kept apprised of the race by the entry of messengers with megaphones. Now they heard the sound of horns that heralded the approach of the first runner. Though disappointed that a Swede was not in the lead, they cheered enthusiastically for McArthur. As he circled the track, a victory wreath was placed around him. One source claims that a spectator told McArthur that Gitsham was five minutes behind and that the leader subsequently slowed his pace somewhat, but McArthur had only recently passed his teammate, and would not be likely to believe that his lead had grown so quickly. McArthur finished in a time of 2:36:54, collapsing onto the grass after crossing the line. As medical personnel were attending to the victor, Gitsham finished less than a minute behind. The surprise bronze medal winner was American Gaston Strobino, the least of the hopes on the strong American team that was defeated by the field, the weather, and perhaps their own misguided coaching.

After the race McArthur received offers to turn professional, but he chose instead to retire from running. Gitsham returned to track running in South Africa, but he would be back for the 1920 Olympic Marathon in Antwerp. On that day in July, though, the two countrymen were champions, and they rode through Stockholm waving the Union Jack to the cheering crowds.

The dreadful conditions, especially the heat, that had marked many of the early Olympic marathons, finally took the ultimate toll during the Stockholm race. A twenty-one-year-old Portuguese runner named Francisco Lazaro collapsed near the end of the race. He was rushed to the hospital, suffering from sunstroke and heart trouble, and he died the following day. He was the first athlete ever to die as a result of participation in the Olympic Games. Lazaro's death cast a gloom over the end of the Stockholm Games, but after the Olympics, Swedish athletic leaders sponsored a special display at the stadium which raised nearly four thousand dollars for Lazaro's family.

Another athlete forced to drop out because of the heat was Shizo Kanakuri of Japan. Kanakuri pledged that he would finish the race, though, and eventually he did. In 1967 he came to Stockholm and ran the final lap around the track of the Olympic Stadium. His unofficial time for the marathon: fifty-four years, eight months, six days, eight hours, thirty-two minutes, and twenty seconds.

In spite of the sad pall cast over the Stockholm Games by the death of Lazaro, these Olympics did much to entrench the Olympic movement after the controversies of London and the problems of St. Louis and Paris. It is fortunate that the movement was now firmly in place, for it, along with everything else in Western culture, was about to experience a severe shock—World War I.

7

The Games of the VII Olympiad: Antwerp, 1920

The Games of 1916 had been scheduled to take place in Berlin, but with the outbreak of World War I, they were cancelled. To help preserve the Olympic movement, the headquarters of the IOC was moved to the neutral country of Switzerland where they were established near Pierre de Coubertin's new home in Lausanne, and where they remain to this day. The 1920 Games had been planned for Budapest, but after the war, it was thought inappropriate to extend the invitation to either the Germans or the Hungarians to host the Games because they were viewed as the aggressors in the war, so the IOC awarded the Games to the city of Antwerp, Belgium.

The Belgians did their best to host the Games, a remarkable effort considering the devastation remaining from the war, which had ended only twenty months prior to the start of the competition. Though most events were not well attended, because Belgians could afford very little and could not spend money on sporting tickets, all agreed that the hosts had done the best that could be expected under the circumstances. The Antwerp Games were the first over which the five-ringed Olympic flag flew. The flag was a gift from the city of Antwerp and the same flag still flies over an Olympic stadium every four years. The 1920 Games also featured the introduction of the athletes oath, taken by one athlete in the name of all competitors. In spite of these symbols of unity, Germany and Austria, enemies of the Allies in the recent war, were not invited to participate in the Antwerp Games.

The marathon was contested on August 22 beginning just after 4:00 P.M., and the runners had a chance to compete in the first cool Olympic Marathon ever. A rain served to improve conditions for long-distance racing, and the resulting times were excellent, especially considering that this was the longest Olympic Marathon, at over twenty-six and a half miles.

Forty starters from seventeen nations left the Olympic stadium to run on a circular course through the country which would end back at the stadium. Christian Gitsham, the South African who had taken second in the 1912 race, took the early lead in Antwerp. Gitsham had been training on the Antwerp course for several weeks to prepare for the Olympic race. A little over nine miles into the race, he was joined by the Finnish marvel of the 1912 Games, Hannes Kolehmainen, who was hoping to add a marathon gold to the three golds he had won in Stockholm.

Kolehmainen was born on December 9, 1889, the youngest of three long-distance running brothers. He ran his first marathon when he was only seventeen, and had run eight marathons by the end of 1909. For the next decade, though, he concentrated on shorter races, running only one marathon—Boston in 1917. Beginning in 1913, he lived for several years in the United States, where he won five national championship races at various distances and was married in Brooklyn in 1914. In 1920 he won a marathon in New York to qualify for the Finnish Olympic team.

Gitsham and Kolehmainen ran together for some miles, but Kolehmainen pulled ahead at about the seventeen-mile mark. Gitsham subsequently dropped out with foot trouble as a result of a torn shoe, and there was much talk that he had trained too hard, not leaving enough reserve for the race. Although Jüri Lossmann of Estonia closed the gap that Kolehmainen had opened up, he was unable to catch the Finn, who won by some 70 yards, the closest finish of any Olympic Marathon yet run. Kolehmainen's time was a stunning 2:32:35, more than four minutes faster than the previous Olympic best, which had been run on a much shorter course. The time was also a three-and-a-half-minute improvement on the world record for the marathon distance which had been set seven years earlier. Kolehmainen's victory became all the more remarkable when the course was remeasured and determined to be over six hundred yards too long. On a properly measured course, Kolehmainen might have had a chance to be the first man to run a marathon in under 2:30, a feat that would not be officially achieved for another fifteen years. Kolehmainen returned to Finland after the Olympics, but he did compete in the 1924 Paris Olympic Marathon, a race he failed to finish. In 1928 he dropped out of the Finnish trial race and ended his competitive career.

As for Jüri Lossmann, who had almost caught the winner at the tape, he later claimed that if he had received any support from his teammates he could have won the gold. But the Estonian team chose that day to take an excursion, rather than watch the race and cheer on their teammate. Lossmann did not speak any language but Estonian and so when someone along the course made a signal to him, he believed there was still over a mile to go in the race when, in fact, the stadium was in sight. Had Lossmann made his final surge a bit earlier, he might well have made up the deficit and caught Kolehmainen for the gold. He returned for the marathon in Paris in 1924, finishing tenth.

With a surge late in the race that moved him up from well back in the pack, Valerio Arri of Italy took the bronze medal. He was so eager to demonstrate his energy at the finish line that he turned three cartwheels. This was a refreshing change from previous finishes where contestants appeared near death. In fact, all the finishers crossed the line in good health, partly due, no doubt, to the weather.

The Antwerp Games saw the Olympic debut of the great Finnish long-distance runner, Paavo Nurmi, who won a silver medal in the 5,000 meters and a gold in the 10,000 meters. Nurmi would take on the title of "Flying Finn," which some had given to Hannes Kolehmainen. But for Kolehmainen, the Antwerp marathon was the crowning achievement of a spectacular Olympic career.

The race was also the last Olympic Marathon to cover a distance other than the standard 26 miles, 385 yards. With the improvement of times and the good health of the contestants it represented another step forward for the race.

Hannes Kolehmainen would run in only two more marathons, and would not finish either one. He died on January 11, 1966.

8

The Games of the VIII Olympiad: Paris, 1924

In 1924 the Olympic Games returned to Paris, where Pierre de Coubertin hoped they would be given better treatment than in 1900. Indeed, Paris did redeem itself, hosting a splendid Games. In contrast with the empty stands at the 1900 Games, the art of scalping Olympic tickets was invented in Paris in 1924. These were the games of Harold Abrahams and Eric Liddell of Great Britain (as immortalized with some Hollywood additions in *Chariots of Fire*), but most of all, they were the games of the Finns, and especially Paavo Nurmi. The Finnish team won ten gold medals in the track and field competition, with Nurmi taking four, despite being kept out of the 10,000 meters by his team officials.

The marathon was held on July 13, and not surprisingly, the weather was hot. For this reason the start of the race was delayed from 3:00 P.M.until 5:00 P.M. in hopes that the air would be cooler by then. The course measured the now standard 26 miles 385 yards; that length had been adopted by the International Amateur Athletic Federation (IAAF) in 1921. The IAAF had been formed in 1912, and was responsible, as it still is, for the rules governing international track and field competitions.

Running in Paris for the United States was once again Clarence DeMar, who had competed in 1912. DeMar had won his third Boston marathon in a row, and his fourth over all (he would eventually win seven), earlier that year. In 1924, Boston, like the Olympics, adopted the standard distance of

26 miles 385 yards, and DeMar's sub–2:30 victory automatically earned him a spot on the Olympic team.

DeMar, though, was concerned about the forced group workouts and other problems that plagued the 1912 team, so he approached head coach Lawson Robertson to ensure he would be able to train as he saw fit. Robertson agreed that DeMar should train any way he liked. Mike Ryan, the captain DeMar had found so overbearing in 1912, was now the marathon coach, and DeMar contacted him by letter with a similar demand. Ryan wrote back agreeing to DeMar's request. When the team left for France, the American officials told the athletes they would train together, but Robertson assured DeMar that this ultimatum did not apply to him. In France, DeMar trained alone, while the other six members of the team trained under Ryan. Just before the race, the American officials decided to enter the alternate, Ralph Williams, in place of the more experienced Carl Linder. Once again, forced training methods and arbitrary decisions undermined much of the U.S. team's morale before the race even started.

The course began at the Colombes stadium in Paris and led to the village of Pontoise and back. The fifty-eight starters, of whom only thirty would finish, represented twenty nations. The French fans, of course, hoped for a Frenchman to win, and much of the early race was led by G. Verger of France who took the lead from Kranis of Greece just after the seven-mile point. But neither Kranis nor Verger would finish the race. Near the halfway mark Verger was passed by Albin Stenroos, from Finland, who had been in sixteenth place in the early stages of the race, but had gradually worked his way through the pack. Stenroos put on a sudden surge to breeze past Verger, who could not respond to the move. Indeed these were enchanted games for the Finns; Stenroos pulled into a lead that grew and grew and was never challenged. He crossed the finish line nearly six minutes ahead of the second place runner.

Clarence DeMar had been running in third place for much of the race, but when Verger began to falter, DeMar moved into second. With Stenroos so far ahead of the field, DeMar was running for silver. But he could not hold off a late charge by Romeo Bertini of Italy, who passed him to take the silver. Clarence DeMar finished third, winning his only Olympic marathoning medal, a bronze.

Stenroos, a sewing machine salesman from Helsinki, was born on February 24, 1889. He had begun his athletic career as a wrestler before he turned to running. At eighteen he had set national records in the 5,000 and 10,000 meters. He ran two marathon races on the track in his early years but then chose to concentrate on the shorter distances. He won a bronze medal in the 10,000 meters race in Stockholm in 1912. Some time after that, he fell and suffered a broken leg, and it was assumed his running days were over. But he began his training as soon as the leg had healed. He set a world record at thirty kilometers in 1915, but after that he competed less and less until, in 1918, he stopped running altogether. In 1921, Stenroos returned to running, and by 1923 he had set another world record, this time at twenty kilometers. Still, he did not run in a marathon race from 1909 until he finished second in the Finnish Olympic trial race on May 18, 1924. When he crossed the finish line in Paris in 1924, he was thirty-five years old and running on a once broken leg, yet never since has anyone won an Olympic Marathon by such a wide margin. He would go on to set another thirty kilometer world record and would live and race in America until his retirement in 1928, when he failed to qualify for the Olympic team.

In the stands cheering Stenroos were Paavo Nurmi, Vilho Ritola, and the rest of the Finnish team. Between them, Nurmi and Ritola had won every race on the track from 1,500 meters to 10,000 meters. With the win by Stenroos in the marathon, the Finns did what no other team has done before or since—sweeping every distance race in the Games. Other members of the team later said that Stenroos was the most honored member of the team, for his victory, unlike those by Nurmi and Ritola, had not been expected.

Following the race, several members of the American team drafted a letter to U.S. Olympic officials asking that the job of marathon coach be eliminated and threatening to sit out future Olympics if it were not. Though the officials never replied to the letter, there was no marathon coach on the 1928 squad, when Clarence DeMar returned at age forty for his final Olympic Marathon, capping a sixteen-year career of participating in the Games.

9

The Games of the IX Olympiad: Amsterdam, 1928

By the time the Amsterdam Olympics opened in 1928, the success and popularity of the Paris Games had left little doubt in anyone's mind that the Olympic movement had arrived to stay. The uncertainty of the early Olympiads that had led to rumors of the downfall of the movement was gone at last. Unfortunately, Pierre de Coubertin was gone as well. Now retired as president of the IOC, Coubertin was not well and remained home for the first time since 1904. He did send a message to the Opening Ceremonies, though, saying farewell to those gathered to celebrate the Games. Coubertin's prediction of his own demise was premature, however. He lived until 1937.

The Amsterdam Games featured several Olympic innovations, including the lighting of a torch at the Olympic stadium, and the inclusion of women in the track and field competition (they had previously competed in such "appropriate" sports as golf, tennis, and diving). Both Coubertin and Pope Pius XI opposed this change. The women who competed on the track were required to wear shorts that came within twelve centimeters (about four inches) of their knees. The marathon was considered too difficult for women, a misconception that would linger for several more decades. The longest race the women competed in was the 800 meters.

The marathon was started just after 3:00 P.M. on August 5, and featured sixty-eight runners from twenty-three nations. The American contingent included Clarence DeMar and Joie Ray, who had failed to medal in the middle distances in two previous Olympics and had decided to move up to the marathon. The course, as might be expected in a low country, was level most of the way. It began in the Amsterdam stadium, passing through the "Olympic gate" into the country where it went along a towpath next to a canal and eventually circled back to the stadium.

The lead changed hands several times in the first half of the race, but the primary pacesetters were Joie Ray, Martti Marttelin of Finland, and Kane-matsu Yamada of Japan. Ray led at the halfway mark, but was passed by Yamada and his teammate Seiichiro Tsuda. These three ran near each other for much of the second half of the race, but two lesser known runners, Boughèra El Ouafi, an Algerian born runner competing for France, and Miguel Plaza Reyes of Chile, gradually moved up on the lead trio. Plaza, a newsboy from Santiago, had run much of the race just behind El Ouafi, as he had in Paris four years earlier. In Paris the strategy resulted in a sixth place finish, just ahead of El Ouafi. This time, though, the strategy led to a medal. Though they had trailed the pack by a significant margin in the early stages of the race, the two men began passing the leaders in the final three miles. With under two miles to go, the Algerian was in second place and the Chilean in third, with only Yamada still in front of them. They overtook Yamada just outside the stadium, and El Ouafi sprinted ahead to win the race by about twenty-six seconds, in a time of 2:32:57. He then saluted the honor guard that had been assembled to receive him at the finish before retiring to change into his street clothes. Martti Marttelin of Finland also passed Yamada near the end of the race, edging the Japanese runner by twenty-seven seconds for the bronze medal. Joie Ray finished fifth, after suffering problems with a leg muscle near the end of the race. The Amster-dam race thus became the first Olympic Marathon in which the first five finishers represented five different countries, a fact that further established the international appeal of the race.

El Ouafi, born in 1899, had not begun running until he was twenty-three. He had been a member of the French Colonial Army but now lived in Paris working as an auto mechanic. After his seventh-place finish in the Paris marathon, he ran only sporadically until 1927, when he began training for the Olympics. After a series of races in 1928 at various distances, only one of which he won, El Ouafi won the national marathon championship in July, just as he had in 1924. As in 1924, he had peaked just in time for the Olympics. El Ouafi became a professional after the 1928 Olympics, defeat-ing Joie Ray in a Madison Square Garden marathon reminiscent of those run between John Hayes and Dorando Pietri.

For his part, Miguel Plaza Reyes was so thrilled with his silver medal effort that he took a Chilean flag offered him by a countryman and circled the track in a victory lap—the type of display some early marathoners would have found impossible because of their over-exhaustion. Plaza continued to race and at the age of 32, in 1933, won the South American half-marathon title.

In his final Olympic race, Clarence DeMar, who won seven Boston marathons over a period of nearly twenty years, could manage no better than twenty-seventh.

A week later, the medals for the track and field competitions were handed out. Queen Wilhelmina of Holland presented the gold medals, Prince Hendrik the silver, and Count Henri Baillet-Latour, president of the IOC, the bronze.

El Ouafi was largely forgotten until the victory of another Algerian-born Frenchman in the 1956 Olympic Marathon recalled his story. At that time he was sought out by journalists, who discovered that he was unemployed and living in poverty in Paris. A fund raising effort was undertaken by French sportsmen to help the runner who had brought glory to their flag in Amsterdam. Three years later, El Ouafi died in a family quarrel at the age of sixty. But for one brief shining moment he was champion of the greatest challenge the Olympic Games has to offer.

The sad story of El Ouafi's life embodies, however, something of the true spirit of the Olympic Games—that on these fields of competition and during these brief times in history one can find glory, honor, valor, victory, and above all peace, even in a world that is too often filled with war, poverty, and hatred. Coming as they did in the midst of a great economic depression, the Olympic Games of 1932 would serve, once again, to remind the world of the escapist nature of the Olympic dream.

10

The Games of the X Olympiad: Los Angeles, 1932

The Olympics returned to the United States in 1932, and this time the host city was Los Angeles. Despite being held in the midst of a worldwide depression (twenty teams were unable to participate because of financial difficulties) the Games were a great success. On the track, Olympic records were set in every event but one, and the competition in other arenas was superb as well. Los Angeles had built magnificent facilities for the competition. In fact, the coliseum in which the track events were held was used as the Olympic stadium again in 1984. The crowds were huge and among the most sportsmanlike ever seen at any Olympics. At one point, when the crowd believed an American runner had been cheated, their boos quickly turned to applause when the public address announcer reminded them that the foreigners were their guests.

For the first time, all the athletes stayed together in an Olympic village, an idea that was scorned by many at the start of the Games and universally acclaimed by the Closing Ceremonies. Since 1932, all Olympic host cities have housed athletes in an Olympic village.

The long-distance events were clouded somewhat by the disqualification of Paavo Nurmi three days before the Opening Ceremonies. The IAAF claimed that Nurmi had received compensation in excess of his expenses while racing in Europe, thus making him ineligible to compete as an amateur. Nurmi had won nine golds and twelve medals overall in the previous three

Olympics, but his days as an Olympic competitor were now over. Prior to the Games, he had been considered a favorite to win the marathon.

In a race held on the Olympic Marathon course earlier in the summer and sponsored by the *Los Angeles Times*, the early leader was Juan Carlos Zabala of Argentina, who led by a remarkable eight and a half minutes when he developed foot problems and his trainer forced him to drop out. If Zabala could make it through the Olympic race, he would certainly be considered one of the leading contenders. Albert Michelsen of the United States had won the *Times* Marathon, and was considered America's best hope at the Games.

Zabala was running not only for himself, but also for his coach, Andrew Stirling. Stirling, a physical education teacher from Scotland, saw Zabala run at age thirteen and immediately recognized his talent. Zabala was an orphan, and Stirling virtually adopted him, training him to become a world class runner. By the time he was twenty, Zabala had won the South American title at 10,000 meters. He then travelled to Europe with Stirling to train for the Olympics. In October of 1931 he set a world record for thirty kilometers. Stirling felt Zabala was finally ready for the marathon, and the young man won his first outing at that distance. Despite having dropped out of the earlier Los Angeles marathon, Zabala felt confident entering the Olympic race.

The marathon was held on August 7, and featured only twenty-nine runners from fifteen countries, the smallest marathon field since the Paris Games of 1900. The course started and finished at the Olympic stadium, winding its way through the neighborhoods of Los Angeles. Zabala had announced before the start that he would win the race, but a number of other runners left the stadium with more quiet confidence.

In many ways, the 1932 Olympic Marathon was one of the most competitive ever. The lead changed hands many times, and the finish certainly proved how evenly matched the best runners were on that day. One reason for the high caliber of competition may have been the excellent running conditions—only eight runners did not finish the race. Both the weather and the road surfaces were conducive to good marathoning.

Zabala took the early lead, and though he was passed briefly by the Mexican runner Margarito Baños he held the lead for most of the first nineteen miles. It looked as though Zabala's prediction of victory would hold true and that the competition at the front of the pack would be minimal. But nearly twenty miles into the race, things began to happen. First Lauri Virtanen of Finland, who had won bronze medals in the 5,000 and 10,000 meter races, sprinted to a lead of several hundred yards. The Finnish long-distance runners had earned respect over the past few Olympiads, and spectators must have suspected another Finnish medal was in the making.

Virtanen's move seemed to act as a catalyst, and runners throughout the field who had been biding their time began to vie for position. Duncan Wright of Great Britain was the first to overtake Virtanen and move into the lead, which he did at about twenty miles—a move that the British team had calculated before the race. By twenty-three miles, Virtanen, exhausted by the pace, dropped out of the race. His countryman Armas Toivonen had moved into third place behind Zabala, who trailed Wright by a minute.

Then, Wright began to fade and Zabala moved back into the lead, this time being chased by another British runner, Sam Ferris, who had finished eighth in Amsterdam. Ferris sprinted after Zabala, but he was too late. According to one story, Ferris had toured the course earlier, picking out a milk billboard as the spot to begin his final sprint. The crowds in bleachers along the course made it impossible for him to see his landmark, though, and he waited too long to surge after Zabala. The Argentinean entered the stadium with a one-minute lead. He was clearly exhausted as he circled the track in his blue running outfit and white hat, which he barely had the energy to wave at the crowd. Behind him, however, Ferris was running strong followed by Toivonen and Wright. The crowd was treated to a rare moment as four marathoners circled the track simultaneously. Their positions held and Zabala won the gold as he had predicted, but his exhaustion was total, and he collapsed on the track after the finish. Clearly Ferris would have overtaken him had the race extended another few hundred yards. Zabala, still only twenty, became the youngest man ever to win the Olympic Marathon, a distinction he enjoys to this day.

Zabala set a new Olympic record with his time of 2:31:36, and the first four finishers crossed the line in a span of one minute and five seconds. American Albert Michelsen could manage no better than seventh. Though there were no changes of the lead at the last second in this race, it was tremendously competitive, with at least four men in serious contention up to the last few hundred yards. For the fourth Olympiad in a row, Finland won a marathon medal, this time the bronze that went to Armas Toivonen. Seiichiro Tsuda of Japan, who had played an important role in the Amsterdam race of 1928, finished fifth in Los Angeles followed by Eun-Bae Kim of Korea. Kim was forced to run under the Japanese flag, as Korea was at that time under Japanese occupation. That fact, though perhaps lost in the flurry of record breaking performances in Los Angeles, would have a serious bearing on the next Olympic Marathon and on the future of the Olympic movement.

I I

The Games of the XI Olympiad: Berlin, 1936

The Berlin Games of 1936 were the most politically charged Olympic Games in history. The IOC had voted to grant the Games to Berlin in 1931, before Hitler became Chancellor. By the time 1936 arrived, the world situation, as well as the situation in Berlin, had changed completely. Spain was on the brink of civil war; in fact, their team was called home from the Games when the war broke out. Japan had invaded Manchuria, Italy had conquered Ethiopia, and Adolf Hitler had taken over Germany, turned it into a fascist state, and was prepared to imbue the Olympics with his own philosophies of Aryan supremacy and anti-Semitism. The Amateur Athletic Union (AAU) of the United States narrowly voted to send a team to the 1936 Games. A large contingent had lobbied for a boycott to protest Hitler's policies.

The IOC gave Hitler little leeway in setting the rules of the Games. It insisted, for instance, that Jews be allowed to compete on Germany's team and the teams of any other nation, against the will of the Führer. But Hitler knew that the Olympic Games afforded him a tremendous propaganda opportunity, so he complied with the IOC's demands. The Olympics, he felt, would allow him to demonstrate the strength and efficiency of his fascist state, as well as the physical superiority of his "master race" of Aryans.

The Olympic complex was the largest ever built, with room for 110,000 in the Olympic stadium. Estimates of its cost ranged as high as $30 million. The Opening Ceremonies featured the first Olympic flame to be run by relay all the way from Greece. Richard Straus conducted a massive orchestra. For the marathon enthusiast, however, the highlight came when sixty-four-year-old Spiridon Louis, the winner of the first Olympic Marathon in 1896, presented the Führer with an olive branch from the sacred grove of Zeus at Olympia in Greece. Louis was wearing the same traditional Greek costume he had worn at the King's breakfast in 1896. The bitter irony of this presentation of a branch of peace to Adolf Hitler would become evident in the years following the Games and would be compounded by the fact that several Olympic medal winners would perish in the Holocaust.

Hitler's wish that the Games showcase Germany's efficiency was certainly fulfilled; the Germans' superb facilities and magnificent pageant created an Olympics like never before. Hitler's desire to prove the superiority of the Aryan race, however, was soon squelched in dramatic fashion by American Jesse Owens, an African American who won four gold medals in track and field.

Often the marathon race is a reflection of the Games at large, and 1936 was no exception. Just as political conflict colored the Games as a whole, it colored the marathon race in a way it never had before.

The race was run on August 9, and as had become the tradition, it started and finished in the Olympic stadium. The course led out into the countryside along the Havel River. Fifty-six starters represented twenty-seven nations. Among the favorites were the defending champion Juan Carlos Zabala, a Finnish team coached by Paavo Nurmi, and Korean born Sohn Kee Chung, who was racing under the flag of Japan.

Sohn was born in Korea in 1912, but according to Japanese authorities, there was no Korea in 1912. Japan had annexed Korea two years earlier, after their victory in the 1904–1905 Russo-Japanese war. Sohn grew up in a country that was not allowed to have its own identity. Koreans were forced to speak Japanese and change their names to conform to Japanese spelling. But Sohn found a way to escape from the tyranny of Japanese occupation—running.

"The Japanese could stop our musicians from playing our songs," said Sohn. "They could stop our singers and silence our speakers. But they could not stop me from running."[2] As a boy Sohn ran two miles to buy bread for his family each day. He raced against his friends on their bicycles and ice skates. And he ran for the sheer pleasure of running, despite pleas from his mother that he concentrate more on his school work.

In 1931, his running caught the eye of Kim Soo Kee, the track coach at Seoul's Yangjung High School. Yangjung was a private school with a reputation for turning out excellent runners. In fact, two recent graduates had finished in the top ten in the 1932 Olympic Marathon in Los Angeles. Under Kim's coaching, Sohn continued to develop.

On October 10, 1933, at the age of nineteen, Sohn ran his first marathon, winning the race in a time of 2:29:34, less than a minute shy of the world record. Officials later declared that the course on which he had run was short, but in 1935 Sohn entered a marathon on an officially sanctioned course in Tokyo and set a world record of 2:26:42, eclipsing the old mark by over three minutes. But Sohn had not competed internationally, and the 1936 Olympics could give him an opportunity to show his talents to the world. The Japanese authorities insisted that Korea as a country did not exist, therefore to compete in the Olympics, Sohn would have to qualify for the Japanese team.

When the Japanese held their Olympic Marathon trials, Sohn finished second to his countryman and schoolmate Nam Sung Yong. Japanese officials sent the two Koreans, along with the third and fourth place Japanese finishers, on a twelve-day railway journey to Berlin, where they arrived a month and a half before the Games were to start.

In Germany, the Japanese held another trial race, in hopes that a native Japanese runner would outclass the Koreans. In spite of the fact that a Japanese runner allegedly took a short cut during the eighteen-mile race, Nam and Sohn again finished first and second and so would run in the Olympics.

But Sohn would not only be denied the right to run for his own country and under his own flag, he would be denied even his Korean name. He was listed on the official entry forms as Kitei Son of Japan. He had signed the Olympic register with his real name and sketched a small map of Korea next to the entry but, though he told everyone he could of his true nationality, few spectators realized that Sohn Kee Chung of Korea was competing in the marathon.

Sohn did make friends in Germany, though, among them Jesse Owens, the American sprinter who would debunk Hitler's theories of Aryan supremacy. "He was the first black man I had seen with my own eyes," Sohn said later, "and though at first we couldn't understand each other, we practiced together every day and became friends."

The day of the race was hot and much of the course was unshaded. The starter's gun sounded at 3 P.M. and Juan Carlos Zabala jumped to the front of the pack. He had been training in Germany for three months and had become a favorite with the local spectators, who fully expected him to repeat as Olympic champion. Because no German runner seemed likely to challenge for the gold, Zabala, as an Argentine, was treated as almost an adopted German. Zabala led the runners out of the stadium onto the course, which, by now, was quite familiar to him.

Sohn had planned to run with Zabala from the start in an effort to win the gold, but when Zabala set the early pace, Sohn felt it was much too fast for a marathon. He fell into last place and began to think that he might try for fifth place rather than first; a Korean runner had never finished better than sixth in the Olympic Marathon. His goal of reaching fifth was realized soon, as the pack began to weaken and slow almost immediately. Sohn was in fifth place after only three miles. By six miles he had pulled even with Ernie Harper of Great Britain, who had placed twenty-second in the Amsterdam race in 1928. When Sohn started to pick up the pace, Harper used hand signals to convince him to slow down. Sohn and Harper ran together and seemed to be conversing as they ran. By the eleven-mile mark they had moved into second and third place. The two were starting to attract the attention of the crowd—Harper with his perfectly combed hair contrasting with his pained facial expressions and Sohn with his odd Japanese shoes (white cloth with a separate compartment for the big toe).

"We had to buy our own shoes," Sohn said, "so I got the cheapest I could find."

Meanwhile, at the front of the race Zabala was building his lead in an effort to become the first two-time winner of the Olympic Marathon. His lead of one minute thirty seconds at the nine-mile mark had slipped to fifty seconds at halfway through the race, but he built it back to ninety seconds at the fifteen-mile point. But Sohn and Harper began to reel in Zabala as the race wore on. Just past the seventeen-mile point, Sohn passed Zabala, to the shock of the Argentine runner. Zabala was further demoralized when Harper passed him just seconds later. Exhausted by his early pace, Zabala fell, and though he recovered and continued to run, he was unable to remain competitive. Just over two miles later he dropped out of the race. Back in the stadium, a crowd that included Hitler heard updates on the race over the loudspeaker system.

While Zabala struggled and faltered, Sohn pulled away from Harper, running the last five miles of the race alone. So great was his reserve of energy at the end of the race that he sprinted the last one hundred yards in twelve seconds.

"We weren't very scientific about running in those days," said Sohn, "so I had a lot of strength left."

Sohn's margin of victory over second place Harper was more than two minutes, and he set a new Olympic record of 2:29:19, thus becoming the first to run an Olympic Marathon in under 2:30. He had taken off his shoes and disappeared under the stands into the dressing room by the time Harper arrived on the track.

Behind Sohn, the battle was on for silver and bronze. Sohn's teammate, Nam Sung Yong, was running in third place, but a trio of Finnish runners who had run together throughout, attempted to use team tactics to break him. They took turns passing Nam, but the Korean would not be intimidated and eventually pulled away from the Finns and set his sights on Ernie Harper in second place. Harper had developed a bad blister and ran gallantly to hold off Nam's charge. By the end of the race, Harper's shoe had filled with blood, but he had clinched the silver medal, finishing less than ten seconds ahead of the Korean.

When the victory ceremony was held, two Koreans stood on the podium, wreaths of laurel on their heads, but the flag of Japan was raised in the stadium and the national anthem of Japan was played. Both Sohn and Nam lowered their heads in protest.

Sohn later described the medal ceremony as torture, saying he wished he had never come to Berlin. Following the race, Sohn tried to tell the press that he was Korean, but his translator was Japanese and his statements never made it to the outside world. The name Kitei Son would enter the Olympic record books that day, next to the country Japan, to the shame of one of Korea's greatest athletes.

Determined to do something about the situation, Sohn boldly asked for an audience with Hitler. To his shock, the request was granted, but Sohn found it impossible to speak out in the Chancellor's presence. "What I was going to say was, 'Mr. Hitler, I am a man without a country.' But I held back. I don't think he would have understood anyway."

Back in Korea, Sohn's countrymen took tremendous pride in his accomplishment. If the rest of the world did not know he was Korea's first Olympic champion, they did. A newspaper in Seoul printed a picture of Sohn on the victory stand but covered up the Japanese insignia on his uniform. The Japanese authorities subsequently arrested ten staff members and closed down the paper for ten months to punish this action.

The Olympics of 1936 drew to a close, and as they did, the modern Olympic movement experienced its longest hiatus ever. By 1940, the next scheduled Olympic Games, the world would be at war. In ancient times, wars were suspended in order that the Olympic Games could be held. The modern Olympic movement was cursed with the reverse situation, and the Games of 1940 and 1944 would both be cancelled. The politics that had colored the 1936 Games would obliterate the next two Olympiads.

Sohn Kee Chung returned to his country and vowed never to run for Japan again. In fact, he had no choice. Embarrassed by the prospect of a successful Korean athlete, Japanese authorities forced him into retirement. He never ran another marathon. He did become a successful businessman, and following the war carried the flag of South Korea in the Opening Ceremonies of the 1948 Games. He was also a member of the committee that helped convince the IOC to stage the 1988 Games in Seoul.

Sohn, who continued to run for his own pleasure, would run once more before an international audience—an audience bigger even than the million spectators that had lined the roads of Germany in 1936. When the Summer Games of 1988 opened in Seoul, South Korea, seventy-six-year-old Sohn appeared before a television audience of over a billion people, carrying the Olympic flame into the stadium on its final leg from Greece. This time he ran as a Korean in front of his own countrymen, and the world cheered.

12

The Games of the XIV Olympiad: London, 1948

The 1940 Olympic Games had been awarded to Tokyo, but by 1938 the Japanese realized that they were much too busy with their war in China to be able to spare time, men, and money for the sponsorship of the Games, so they declined the honor. The IOC promptly awarded the Games to Helsinki, but by 1940 World War II was raging and all thoughts of Olympic Games were gone.

The 1944 Games had been scheduled for London, but they too disappeared into the shadows of war. As soon as the hostilities ended, however, the IOC met in London and voted to hold the 1948 Games in that city. Like Antwerp in 1920, London would serve as a symbol of the severity of the recent conflict and the peace that was represented by the Olympic Games would be especially poignant in the bombed out remnants of the British capital.

Even with three years to prepare, the British were not able to host the sort of no-expense-spared festivities they had in 1908. The White City Stadium had been destroyed by the bombs of the Luftwaffe. With money and resources in scarce supply, the British converted Wembley Stadium's soccer field into a track and field arena and transformed Royal Air Force barracks into an Olympic village. Though still restricted to severe rations in the light of post-war shortages, the British people turned out by the tens of thousands to watch the Games. Even on rainy days, Wembley Stadium was nearly filled to its capacity of eighty-two thousand. After a twelve-year hiatus for the Games—from which critics claimed they would never recover—the austere Olympics of London served to reinstate the Games at the forefront of international competition.

The Games of 1948 will be remembered for the feats of seventeen-year-old Bob Mathias who won gold in the decathlon and, more importantly for marathon fans, for the Olympic debut of the great distance runner Emil Zátopek. At age twenty-seven, Zátopek, an army lieutenant from Czechoslovakia, won the gold medal in the 10,000 meters and the silver in the 5,000 meters. Despite Zátopek's atrocious running form, in the course of three Olympiads he would become the next Paavo Nurmi.

If the Olympic venues in London in 1948 were in no way comparable to those of the London Games of 1908, the marathon was. Indeed, in the final lap of the race spectators feared they were watching a repeat of the famous ordeal of Dorando Pietri. But all of that came after twenty-six miles of running on one of the most rugged and challenging courses ever created for Olympic competition.

Forty-one runners from twenty-one countries took to the road on August 7. Etienne Gailly, a twenty-five-year-old ex-paratrooper from Belgium who had participated in the final assault against Germany, took the early lead, pulling ahead at about the six-mile mark. Gailly had made a promise to himself at the beginning of the race that if he was standing at the finish he would win a medal. At fifteen miles he led by forty seconds. But Gailly had never run a marathon. The longest race in which he had competed was just over twenty miles, and it was at about the twenty mile mark that he was passed by Yoon-Chil Choi of Korea. Shortly thereafter, Gailly slipped to third place as he was passed by Delfo Cabrera.

Cabrera was a twenty-nine-year-old fireman from Argentina, and the least of the Argentinean hopes for the marathon. Like Gailly, Cabrera was running his first marathon. Born in 1919, Cabrera had won a national title in 1940 in the 1,500 meters. In 1946 he won the South American 10,000 meter title, but no one considered him a serious threat at the marathon distance. By the twenty-two mile point, Choi led by twenty-eight seconds over Cabrera, with Gailly hanging on to third place and Eusebio Guinez, another Argentine, fourth.

As the race wore on, the battle for the lead tightened. First, Choi was unable to summon any more energy and dropped out, leaving Cabrera in the lead. Tom Richards, a thirty-eight-year-old nurse from Wales running under the flag of Great Britain moved into third, overtaking Guinez. With three miles to go, Cabrera's lead was only five seconds over Gailly. With half a mile to go to the stadium, Gailly had moved back into the lead and

Cabrera trailed by fifty yards with Richards following another fifty yards behind him.

When Gailly entered the stadium, a gasp went up from the crowd, and anyone who had witnessed the ordeal of Dorando Pietri forty years earlier must have been stricken with déja vu. Gailly was clearly in the final throes of exhaustion. He leaned badly to one side and staggered slowly around the track, his eyes glazed over. Gailly managed to stay upright, though, and must certainly had hoped to avoid any interference the likes of which disqualified Pietri. With Gailly partway around the track, Cabrera entered the stadium, running strong and hard. He overtook Gailly quickly and breezed across the finish line to win an unexpected gold in a time of 2:34:51.

But Gailly struggled on. Richards was the next to enter the stadium, and he too had no trouble in passing Gailly and earning the silver medal, only sixteen seconds behind Cabrera. The crowd held its breath as Gailly still limped towards the finish line, and gasped when he collapsed on the track with only sixty yards separating him from a much deserved bronze medal. In a moment, Gailly was back on his feet, and the officials allowed him to continue without assistance. Another runner was now two hundred yards behind Gailly and closing quickly. The spectators yelled their encouragement to Gailly and, less than thirty seconds after Richards had finished, Gailly finally crossed the line, and the crowd cheered his dramatically earned bronze medal as much as they had Cabrera's gold or their own countryman's silver. Gailly was carried off the track on a stretcher, but he had kept his promise. Though barely standing at the race's end, he had won a medal.

The finish of the 1948 London marathon represented a sort of cosmic retribution for the confusion in 1908. To any 1948 spectator familiar with the 1908 race, Gailly's bronze medal was won for a brave runner from Belgium, for that tiny country of his home, ravaged now by two wars, and for a small Italian man named Dorando Pietri.

13

The Games of the XV Olympiad: Helsinki, 1952

Helsinki, Finland had originally been awarded the Olympic Games in 1940 after Tokyo bowed out. Twelve years later, the Helsinki Games finally opened. The Finns, who had so dominated long-distance running in recent decades, won few medals but many hearts. Appropriately, the double Olympic torch was lit by two of the greatest of the Finnish distance runners, Paavo Nurmi and Hannes Kolehmainen. The Scandinavian hospitality restored the Olympics to their former glory, as did the participation of a record sixty-nine nations. Especially notable was the entry of the Soviet Union, a country that had not competed in the Olympics since its creation following the Russian revolution of 1917.

Much speculation surrounded the participation of athletes from the previously isolated communist country, but the athletes impressed the world, winning twenty-two gold medals. While Cold War tensions threatened to turn the press coverage of the Olympics into that of a dual meet between the United States and the Soviet Union, in Helsinki all was peaceful. Soviet athletes invited Americans and others into their Olympic compound, which was separate from the rest of the Olympic village and near a military base controlled by the Soviets. Though apparently nervous in the presence of foreigners, the Soviets competed with sportsmanship and were welcomed into the Olympic family.

On the track, the star of the 1952 Games was Emil Zátopek. He had nearly pulled off an impressive double victory in the 5,000 and 10,000 meters in

London, failing in the 5,000 by only two-tenths of a second. In Helsinki he won gold in the 10,000 meters easily, smashing the Olympic record by nearly forty-three seconds. The 5,000 meters proved more challenging as Zátopek trailed going into the final turn. He sprinted ahead, though, to win by just under a second, once again setting a new Olympic record. Following his race, he loaned his gold medal to his wife, Dana Zátopková, who was about to begin competition in the javelin throw. With her husband's medal in her bag for good luck, Zátopková set an Olympic record on her first throw and won the gold medal.

With three gold medals in the household, not counting the gold Zátopek had won in the 1948 Games, the Czechoslovakian runner announced that he would compete in the marathon, to be run on July 27, just three days after his 5,000 meter win. Zátopek had never run in a marathon before, but that did not keep him from being a favorite with the crowd.

The press had nicknamed Zátopek "The Beast of Prague," "The Czech Express," and "The Human Locomotive" because of his frightening running style. Each step for the Czech runner looked as though it might be his last. His face was constantly contorted as if in terrible pain, his head rolled wildly, and his arms were held high, as if to clutch at his heart. Anyone who watched Zátopek run for a few steps would assume he was on the point of collapse. And, anyone who had run a marathon knew that such a style wasted valuable energy and was not likely to lead to completion of the race, much less victory. Zátopek, however, was not a runner who dealt in likelihoods.

Emil Zátopek was born the son of a carpenter on September 19, 1922, the same day that his wife Dana was born. He began his running career as a teenager working in a shoe factory prior to World War II. Training was interrupted for Zátopek after the Russian invasion of Czechoslovakia when Emil joined the army. Instead of running on the road or track, he ran in place in his army boots while on guard duty.

Zátopek is known in the running world as one of the primary creators of a new system of training called interval training. The interval trainer runs a short distance very fast, rests briefly with a warm-down jog, then runs the distance again, over and over. Interval training builds both speed and endurance, whereas running long distances at a steady pace is more likely to build endurance only. A typical workout for Zátopek while he was training for Helsinki was five times 200 meters, forty times 400 meters, and five times 200 meters. With such an arduous workout schedule, he felt he was in shape to compete in the three longest races of the 1952 Games. The triple that Zátopek was to attempt had never been accomplished. Only

Hannes Kolehmainen, who won the 5,000 and 10,000 meters in 1912 and the marathon in 1920, had even come close.

The marathon began at 3:30 P.M. with two laps around the stadium track. Sixty-six runners represented thirty-two countries. Zátopek had read all the papers, and the papers said that Great Britain's Jim Peters, who had set a world record at the distance only six weeks earlier, would be the man to beat. Because Zátopek was unfamiliar with marathon pacing strategies, he decided to try to keep Peters in sight. The newspaper had also given Zátopek Peters' racing number, and prior to the start he found Peters and introduced himself.

For his own part, Peters would have loved to defeat Zátopek. Peters' first race in the Olympic Games had come in the 10,000 meters in London in 1948, a race that Zátopek had won in style. Peters had finished ninth and had been lapped by Zátopek in the later stages of the race. A victory over the Czech in the marathon might help erase the embarrassment of that moment, which had caused Peters to hide in a temporary retirement. Talked out of retirement by his coach, Peters began to train for the marathon. In 1951 he ran his first two marathons in 2:29 and 2:31, announcing to the marathoning world that he was a force to contend with.

That announcement was heard worldwide on June 11, 1952, when Peters ran the fastest marathon in history, blazing to the finish of the British Olympic qualifying race in 2:20:42. When cynics claimed the course was too short, the course was carefully remeasured and found to be 260 yards too long. Everyone immediately assumed that Peters would be the man to beat in Helsinki, and that beating him would be next to impossible. Peters' countryman Stan Cox had finished the British race in a time of 2:21:42, and was considered a lock to win the silver medal. Never before had the results of the marathon been considered such a foregone conclusion.

When the race began, Peters dashed to the front of the pack at a tremendous pace. Like Zátopek, he used speed in his training. Rather than interval training, however, Peters preferred to run distances of five to ten miles at a race speed of around five minutes to five minutes fifteen seconds per mile. Peters had been afraid that other runners might try to box him in to keep the pace slow, hence his mad dash to the front. By the end of the two laps around the stadium, Peters had built a one hundred yard lead. Zátopek was frightened by the fast pace, yet he felt he must keep in contact with Peters if he was to have any chance of winning. Winning was exactly what Zátopek had in mind—he later said that he wouldn't have entered the race if he didn't think he could win.

So Zátopek and the Swedish runner Gustaf Jansson kept Peters in sight. Though Peters blazed through the first ten kilometers in 31:55, Zátopek and

Jansson were only sixteen seconds back, with Stan Cox following eight seconds behind them. At the ten-mile mark, Zátopek and Jansson caught up with Peters. The three ran together briefly, with Jansson lagging only a few steps behind the other two. Zátopek felt tired, but he knew he must keep up with the leaders. They opened up a lead of more than a minute on Cox and Reinaldo Gorno, an Argentine who had moved into fifth place. Close to the halfway point Zátopek asked Peters, in English, if the pace was too fast. Peters claimed later that he said, as a joke, that the pace was too slow. Years later, though, Zátopek claimed that Peters had said merely, "No, it must be this pace." When Zátopek again asked if the pace was right, Peters moved to the other side of the road, apparently wanting to be alone.

"It is a sign of disharmony, of losing too much energy when someone gets nervous like that," said Zátopek later, "I said to myself, [the pace] must not be right."[3]

Peters soon began to drop back, wearied by the blistering pace he had set, and Zátopek and Jansson continued on alone. Meanwhile, Cox had collapsed at the halfway mark and had to be taken away in an ambulance. There would be no one-two finish for the British.

At the fifteen-mile mark, Zátopek began to pull away, opening a slight lead over Jansson. Peters now trailed by nearly half a minute. By the twenty-mile mark, Peters could take it no more. The brutal early pace, along with a drafty nine-hour plane ride he had taken from London to Helsinki, took its toll. As he struggled to find the strength to catch the leaders, his left leg began to cramp up. He hobbled briefly along the side of the road where he encountered Sam Ferris, the Englishman who had won the silver medal in the 1932 race. Ferris shouted his encouragement to his countryman, but after another two hundred yards, Peters could go no further and dropped out of the race. He was taken by ambulance back to the stadium where he would watch the finish.

Zátopek had no trouble shaking Jansson in the final miles of the race, and he entered the stadium to a thunderous ovation from a crowd that had become convinced he could do anything. Indeed it seemed so, for Zátopek had not only scored a triple victory unequaled before or since, but had also shattered the Olympic Marathon record in his first attempt at the distance. His finishing time was 2:23:03, an improvement of more than six minutes over the previous Olympic best. The crowd was adulatory, chanting "Zá-to-pek, Zá-to-pek" in celebration of the third victory by the tenacious Czech.

Zátopek greeted his wife at the finish line, changed into his warm-up jersey, and was eating an apple when the second place runner crossed the line. In the waning stages of the race, Gorno had overtaken Jansson. Gorno's silver medal effort meant that Argentines had finished first or second in three of the last four Olympic marathons. When Gorno crossed the finish line, Zátopek greeted him with a slice of orange. Jansson held on to third place for a bronze medal. So great was the pace that Peters had established and Zátopek had continued that the top six finishers all broke the previous Olympic record. The sixth of those finishers was Delfo Cabrera, who ran more than eight minutes faster than he had in winning the gold medal in London in 1948. After the medal ceremony, Zátopek jogged a victory lap to the tumultuous applause of the adoring Finns. He had truly earned his spot beside their beloved "Flying Finns" Paavo Nurmi and Hannes Kolehmainen in the pantheon of great distance runners.

Jim Peters went on to break the 2:20 barrier in marathoning on June 13, 1953. He won other marathons, often with his teammate Stan Cox finishing second. In 1954, on an extremely hot day in Vancouver, Peters came close to lowering the record even further, but collapsed on the track 200 yards from the finish. His heat stroke was close to fatal, and with the 1956 Olympics scheduled for Melbourne, Australia, where the weather would almost certainly be hot, Peters, who would be thirty-eight years old by then, retired from marathoning owning the world record but no Olympic medal. He did return to Vancouver in 1967, though, to run one final lap around the track and finish the marathon that had almost killed him thirteen years earlier.

Zátopek had proved himself invincible in Helsinki, but he later admitted that after the marathon he could hardly walk for a week so total was his exhaustion. He had developed blisters during the last few miles, and a headache as a result of the noise of excited spectators. Zátopek had won four gold medals and one silver in five races in the 1948 and 1952 Games. When the Olympic flag was lowered over Helsinki, he and the world looked forward to 1956.

14

The Games of the XVI Olympiad: Melbourne, 1956

The Summer Olympics were held in the southern hemisphere for the first time in 1956, when they opened in Melbourne, Australia on November 22. Though winter was approaching in Paris, London, and Rome, the summer sun shone in Melbourne. Once again politics threatened the Games. Three Arab teams refused to attend in protest of Israel's takeover of the Suez Canal, three European countries boycotted because of the Soviet Union's invasion of Hungary (although Hungary sent a full team that quickly became a favorite with the crowd), and China refused to attend because Taiwan had been given official status by the IOC. It is indicative of the important place the Olympics had taken on the world stage that they had become so symbolic politically. In the decades to come, the Games would be plagued by such political protests, but, as they had survived the World Wars, they would survive the boycotts.

Troubles between local and federal governments in Australia led to a late start in the construction of the Olympic sites, and led the IOC to state several times that Rome, the host of the 1960 Games, was better prepared than Melbourne and could be substitute host of the 1956 games if necessary. But the Australians pulled everything together at last, and the Games opened as scheduled in the 102,000-seat Melbourne cricket arena. Despite the small population of Australia, the Games were extremely well attended, with the spacious venues frequently filled to capacity.

On the track, U.S. sprinters won three gold medals, sweeping the 100 meters, 200 meters, and 4 x 100 meters relay. Local favorite Betty Cuthbert of Australia won gold in the same three races in the women's division. Russian distance runner Vladimir Kuts reminded the crowd of Emil Zátopek by winning the 5,000 and 10,000 meter races, but Zátopek did not compete in those events, saving himself for the marathon.

Zátopek was now thirty-four years old. As 1956 dawned, he was determined to keep up his successful running career despite his age. To this end, he vowed to train harder than ever before. He began his Olympic training by running with his wife, Dana, on his shoulders. Though indicative of his tremendous drive and determination, this turned out to be a mistake, as he gave himself a hernia. After missing a whole summer of training and undergoing surgery to repair the hernia, Zátopek entered the Melbourne marathon against his doctor's advice.

Also entered in the race was Algerian-born Frenchman Alain Mimoun O'Kacha. Mimoun was a French war hero during World War II, and by the end of his career he would set thirty-two national records at various distances. He had been injured in the leg while fighting in Italy during the war, but he went on to win four International Cross-Country Championships between 1949 and 1956. Mimoun was quite familiar with the sight of Emil Zátopek, especially his back. Mimoun had finished second to Zátopek in three of his Olympic gold medal races—the 10,000 meters in 1948 and 1952 and the 5,000 meters in 1952. He had also won silver to Zátopek's gold in two races in the World Championships. Determined to triumph over his Czech rival, Mimoun, the perennial also-ran, entered the marathon in Melbourne, though he, like Zátopek four years earlier, had never competed at that distance. A year before the Olympics he had been forced to walk with a cane because of pain in his feet and earlier in the Games he had finished twelfth in the 10,000 meters, so few prognosticators listed him among the marathon favorites.

At the start of the race, Mimoun felt blessed with good omens. A Frenchman had won the marathon in 1900 and twenty-eight years later in 1928. Now, twenty-eight years after that win, he felt it was his turn. He wore his lucky number thirteen and carried with him the happy knowledge that he had just become a father. Surely Zátopek's physical condition must have added somewhat to his confidence as well.

The gun sounded for the start of the Olympic Marathon on December 1, 1956, and then, for the first time in Olympic history, sounded again. There had been a false start. So, the forty-six runners from twenty-three nations lined up again, the gun was fired again, and then the runners began their twenty-six mile journey.

Mimoun ran with the lead pack for the first half of the race, then put on a surge of speed going up a hill just before the midway point. And that was the race. No one chased Mimoun, and by the fifteen-mile mark his lead was nearly a minute. His final margin of victory was about a minute and a half. For the third time in a row, the marathon was won by a runner trying the race for the first time. Mimoun had finally found gold in his third Olympics. His time was 2:25:00, and had he run that time in the marathon four years earlier, he would have won a silver medal, losing out to Emil Zátopek.

Next across the line was Franjo Mihalic of Yugoslavia followed by Finland's Veikko Karvonen. Zátopek finished a respectable sixth, receiving at least as large an ovation from the crowd as the winner. When he crossed the line in 2:29:34, his old competitor Mimoun, who had cheered him on over the last few yards, was there to greet him with a warm embrace. Mimoun later said that Zátopek's hug was better than the gold medal.

Mimoun's marathon career had just begun. In the next ten years, he would win the French championship race six times. At the age of 51, he ran a marathon in 2:34:36.

As for Zátopek, Melbourne was his second and final marathon. Despite running the race only twice, and placing sixth in one of those races, he is remembered as a master of the distance. He ran several shorter races in the next year, but retired completely after winning a cross-country race in Spain in January of 1958. His wife Dana took fourth in the javelin throw in Melbourne, and then returned four years later to win the silver medal in Rome, where she competed in her fourth Olympics at the age of thirty-seven.

Zátopek's running successes had earned him promotions in the Czech army, but, though he was a Communist, he did not support the puppet government set up by Moscow. In 1968, he and his wife participated in the peaceful revolution that overthrew that government. Along with many other prominent and well-educated Czechs, they signed the *Manifesto of 2,000 Words*—a statement of defiance against the Soviet juggernaut. When Russian tanks rolled into Prague that summer, Zátopek confronted an officer and told him the invasion was unjust. But the tanks kept rolling, and when officials found Zátopek's name on the manifesto, he was thrown out of the army and the Communist Party.

Unable to get work because people in Prague were afraid to hire him, Zátopek finally found a job on a geological survey team out in the country-side. He spent long days digging and carrying bags of concrete, often staying in a trailer away from his wife for two weeks at a time. In 1971, under pressure from sports officials and secret police, he signed a document that accepted the current regime, but his life did not change right away. Eventually he was given a chance to travel to various international events, but when he returned home, it was back to the digging.

Finally, in 1975, Zátopek was given a job as a "spy" with the Ministry of Sport. Until his retirement in 1982, he used his multi-lingual ability to read sports journals from all over the world and keep an eye on other countries' coaching techniques.

In 1990, following the fall of communism, Zátopek was reinstated in the Czech army and the defense minister apologized for his dismissal twenty-two years earlier. Now Zátopek and his wife enjoy living in a truly free Czechoslovakia for the first time since before World War II.

Zátopek left an indelible mark on Olympic and marathon history, but in 1960 he would be replaced with another symbol of resistance against foreign oppression, and one of the great marathoners of the twentieth century.

15

The Games of the XVII Olympiad: Rome, 1960

In 394 A.D. the Roman Emperor Theodosius passed a decree outlawing all non-Christian celebrations, effectively ending the celebration known as the Olympic Games, which had taken place every four years for centuries. Rome played its part in the new Olympic movement 1,566 years after that decree, and the organizers, well aware of the rich historical implications, planned a spectacle that blended ancient and modern elements in breathtaking perfection.

The Italian Olympic Committee was given a percentage of the take from the weekly lottery on professional soccer, and as a result had more than $30 million to work with, enabling them to spare no expense in making these the most lavish Games imaginable. But despite the sparkling modern arenas such as the Palazzo della Sport where boxing and basketball finals were held, the Games had more than a little ancient color.

The Basilica of Maxentius played host to wrestling competitions, just as it had in ancient times, and the gymnasts, like their ancient counterparts, competed in the Terme di Caracala. These sites were a bit worse for the wear after nearly 2,000 years without hosting a competition, but the ruins provided a dramatic backdrop for the Games.

Because of the hot Italian summers, the start of the Games was pushed back to August 25. Thanks to an innovation called videotape, audiences in the United States had their first opportunity to watch same-day prime time coverage of Olympic events. Videotape was flown from Rome to New York by the CBS television network for broadcast each evening. No one took greater advantage of this new medium than a young boxer named Cassius Clay, whose witty poetry and banter as well as his gold medal made him the best known athlete at the Games. Later, as Muhammad Ali, he would become the best-known athlete in the world, and he would remain associated with the Olympic Games, lighting the torch at the opening ceremonies in Atlanta in 1996.

The culmination of these ancient and modern Games was the marathon race, held on September 10, and no other event took such great advantage of Rome's history and architecture. For the first time in Olympic history, the race would neither start nor end in the Olympic Stadium. Also for the first time, the race would be held at night. The course began at the Campidoglio on Capitoline Hill, a beautiful square designed by Michelangelo, and wound its way through the sites of Rome. Because the starting time was 5:30 P.M., the last miles of the race would take place in darkness, with the way being lit by torches held by Roman soldiers. The final stages of the race would be run on the Appian way, where Roman legions had marched millennia before. The finish was at the majestic Arch of Constantine. The setting was enough to make this race a dramatic event, but even had it been held in the most ordinary of places, this would have been a race like no other.

Among the record field of sixty-nine runners from thirty-five countries who awaited the starter's gun at the base of an 1,800-year-old statue of Marcus Aurelius were Sergie Popov of the Soviet Union, who held the world record of 2:15:17; Barry Magee of New Zealand; Aurele Vandendriessche, the Belgian national champion for five years running; Arthur Keily of Great Britain, the first Englishman to run under 2:20 since Jim Peters; and Moroccan Rhadi ben Abdesselem. With so many strong runners to watch, few spectators took much notice of a twenty-eight-year-old Ethiopian who also stood at the starting line. The only thing about his appearance that might have caused comment was his lack of shoes. Abebe Bikila would run the Olympic Marathon in bare feet.

Bikila, a slim almost frail looking man, was born in the Ethiopian mountains on August 7, 1932, the day that the Olympic Marathon was contested in Los Angeles. His father was a shepherd. Bikila became a private in Haile Selassie's Imperial Body Guards. As such, he had been sent to train at a camp set up following World War II by the Ethiopian government. The camp, which was run by Swedish coach Onni Niskanen, was intended to produce athletes. Bikila, who started running at age twenty-four, met Niskanen there in 1959 and the coach immediately recognized the young man's talent. In the thin air of 6,000 feet, Niskanen put Bikila and others through rugged workouts, including cross-country runs of up to twenty miles and interval workouts of 1,500 meter repeats. Bikila and the other soldiers at the camp would often run workouts over the rough terrain in bare feet.

Because of the isolation of his country from the rest of the world, no one much noticed when Bikila won his first marathon in July of 1960 in Addis Ababa. The Ethiopians were not, after all, Olympic threats. They had competed in the Olympics for the first time in 1956 when their delegation of twelve athletes was among the first East Africans ever to join the Games. None of the Ethiopians won a medal. Bikila's time in the Addis Ababa marathon was 2:39:50—not particularly impressive and certainly not fast enough make him a threat to compete for a medal in the Olympics two months later. In August, Bikila ran another marathon in the Ethiopian capital, this time finishing in 2:21:23. Niskanen was confident that Bikila would win at the Olympics, especially when the runner continued to improve after coming to Rome. Had anyone been paying attention to Bikila and had they considered not only the dramatic improvement in his time but also the fact that both his previous marathons were run at high altitude with only a one-month rest between races, Bikila might have drawn some attention when he started off on the historic course of the Rome race. But the Ethiopian was virtually unknown when the race started, and it would take more than bare feet to introduce himself to the world.

Shortly after the start of the race, a group of four runners moved to the front—Keily of Great Britain, Vandendriessche of Belgium, Rhadi of Morocco (who had placed fourteenth in the 10,000 meters two days earlier), and the barefooted Bikila. Bikila had tried running on the Roman roads in shoes, but found that they pinched his feet, so he decided to run without them. By the six-mile mark, people were beginning to notice.

Two more runners caught up with the lead group at about six miles, but world record holder Popov remained in the second group of runners about thirty seconds back. By the twelve-mile mark, the two African runners had broken away from the others and were running together thirty seconds ahead of Vandendriessche and forty-five seconds ahead of Keily. Part of Bikila's strategy had been that he would not take the lead before the twelve-mile mark. Now, at that very point, he seemed to have narrowed his field of competitors to one. In the next few miles, Magee and Popov broke away from their pack and overtook Vandendriessche and Keily, but they still trailed the two African runners by more than three minutes.

At the eighteen-mile mark, the course turned onto the Appian Way. The duel between Bikila and Rhadi continued at the front, but Popov and Magee were closing the gap ever so slightly. By twenty-one miles, Popov had dropped back and Magee continued his pursuit of the leaders alone. By twenty-four miles he had cut the lead to a minute and a half, but time was running out.

Meanwhile the duel for the gold was about to be staged under the light of the torches that now lined the course. A few days earlier Bikila and his coach Onni Niskanen had scouted the course for the perfect place for Bikila to stage his final surge, should anyone still be running with him near the finish. The fact that they assumed Bikila would be among the leaders near the end of the race was indicative of the confidence they shared with virtually no one else in the world. The last few miles of the course passed by the catacombs and the Church of Quo Vadis where Peter had seen a vision of Christ nearly 2,000 years earlier. Just over one mile from the finish, at the foot of an incline, Niskanen and Bikila found what they were looking for. With the Arch of Constantine nearly in sight, the runners would pass the obelisk of Axum. To most spectators the obelisk was just another ancient artifact, but to Bikila it held special significance, for it had been plundered from Ethiopia by invading Italian troops.

Although Rhadi attempted to break away from Bikila in the closing stages of the race, Bikila stayed with him, and as the two passed the obelisk of Axum, Bikila put on a surge that the Moroccan was unable to answer. In the final mile of the race he outran Rhadi by twenty-five seconds, dodging a driver who had swerved his motor scooter onto the course sixty yards from the finish. Bikila finished with a time of 2:15:16.2, winning the gold medal, breaking Popov's world record by eight tenths of a second, and lowering the Olympic record by nearly eight minutes.

Italian papers the next morning commented that while it took one of Mussolini's armies to conquer Addis Ababa, it took only a single foot soldier from the Emperor's Bodyguard to conquer Rome.

Bikila's gold was the first Olympic medal won by a black African and that, combined with Rhadi's silver, signaled the beginning of the domination of distance running by Africans. Magee took the bronze, finishing about two minutes behind Bikila. In the waning stages of the race, Popov faded and was overtaken by his countryman Konstantin Vorobiev, the two Soviets finishing fourth and fifth.

Bikila was an instant celebrity. In his home country and around the world he was heralded as the Ethiopian who conquered Rome. The following year he competed in and won marathons on the original Marathon to Athens course, in Osaka, Japan, and in Czechoslovakia. Following the last of these races, in October of 1961, he returned to Ethiopia, still in possession of the world record, and was not heard from for nearly two years.

In 1963 Bikila ran in the Boston Marathon, along with his countryman Mamo Wolde. For the first time in his career, he lost. He finished fifth, behind a course record performance by Vandendriessche of Belgium. Mamo Wolde finished in twelfth place. Once again, Bikila returned to his army duties in Ethiopia, and the world wondered if they would ever see him race again.

16

The Games of the XVIII Olympiad: Tokyo, 1964

The Olympic Games had first been awarded to Tokyo in 1940, but the Japanese subsequently declined the honor because of their war with China. The 1940 Games were never held, due in part to Japanese aggression. By 1964, however, the world was ready to let bygones be bygones, and the Games were scheduled on Asian soil for the first time ever. The Japanese were determined to host a splendid Games—their national pride demanded it—but pulling off such a task would require the virtual rebuilding of Tokyo, still not fully recovered from the firebombs of World War II.

The Japanese spared no expense in building highways, subways, monorails, hotels, and all the other facilities of a modern city. Nearly $3 billion was spent to modernize the city, and another $60 million was spent on the facilities for the Games.

Determined that the Games run smoothly, the Japanese hosted an International Sports Week in Tokyo in 1963 as a sort of dress rehearsal. The dry-run was successful, but the Japanese did not stop planning. With the finishing touches being put on a revitalized city, a full scale rehearsal of the Opening and Closing Ceremonies was held a week before the Games were scheduled to open. Eight thousand high school students acted in the roles of athletes and officials and another 70,000 schoolchildren played the parts of spectators, filling the stands of the new National Stadium outside the gardens of the Meiji Shrine. Further rehearsals were held later in the week to ensure that everything was perfect. Only mother nature could interfere with the meticulous planning of the Japanese, but by opening day the remnants of Typhoon Wilma had blown away, a mild earthquake had been forgotten, and the sun shone brightly in blue skies above the packed stadium.

The highlight of the October 10 Opening Ceremonies was the lighting of the torch by nineteen-year-old Yoshinori Sakai, who had been born in Hiroshima on the day of that city's destruction by an American atomic bomb. No act could better symbolize the concept of triumph over adversity that pervaded the Tokyo Games from the rebuilding of the city to the running of the marathon.

The American team enjoyed spectacular success on the track in Tokyo, inspired perhaps by the victory in the 10,000 meters by Billy Mills. Mills was part Sioux Indian and was virtually ignored by the press prior to the race as having no chance of winning. Running near the leaders for most of the race, Mills surged from behind in the final stretch to win the gold. He improved his personal best time by over fifty seconds and broke the Olympic record in spite of poor track conditions brought on by rainy weather. Later in the Games, Mills would enter the marathon and finish in fourteenth place.

Mills' story was one of triumph against extreme odds, but could a marathoner who had undergone an emergency appendectomy forty days before the race hope to win an Olympic gold medal? Abebe Bikila, the surprise champion from Rome, entered the Tokyo race to answer just that question.

Little had been heard of Bikila for some time after his loss in Boston in 1963. Rumors in the sporting world said that he was running races in Ethiopia, but he also spent much of his time on the Somali border because of Ethiopia's tense relations with that neighbor. On May 31, 1964, though, Bikila ran and won a warm-up marathon in Addis Ababa. His time was 2:23:14, a solid performance considering the altitude, but probably not Olympic calibre.

The Olympic Trial race for Ethiopians was scheduled for August 3, also in the high altitude of Addis Ababa. This time Bikila blazed to a winning time of 2:16:18, a stunning performance at altitude. Even more stunning was the fact that he won the race by only four-tenths of a second over Mamo Wolde. The third place finisher, Demissie Wolde (no relation to Mamo) clocked in at 2:19:30. The Olympic Games, then, would see not one but three world-class marathoners from Ethiopia.

The size of the team was suddenly thrown into doubt, however, when Bikila had to undergo surgery for appendicitis only six weeks before the Olympic race. He made plans to travel to Tokyo with the team, but no one expected him to compete. Bikila could not be conquered by surgery any more than he could be conquered by altitude or world-class competition.

When the field of sixty-eight runners from thirty-five nations assembled in the stadium for the start of the race on October 21, Bikila took his place with the rest of his team, this time wearing white running shoes. He had undertaken no training between the time of his operation and his arrival in Tokyo, but he would compete nonetheless. His coach, Onni Niskanen, had told him to use the same strategy that had worked in Rome—stay with the lead pack until twelve miles, then work on winning the race.

Bikila was loved and admired by the crowd, but he was not a clear favorite, especially given his recent surgery. In fact, the field for the October 21 race seemed wide open. At least fifteen runners had a reasonable chance to win the gold. Australian Ron Clarke decided to run the marathon after competing in three other races that week, including a bronze medal performance in the 10,000 meters. Buddy Edelen of the United States had lowered the world record to 2:14:28 in 1963 only to have Britain's Basil Heatley lower it again by another thirty seconds. The local favorite was Kokichi Tsuburaya of Japan.

When the race began, Ron Clarke dashed to the lead. He was soon joined by Jim Hogan of Ireland and before the four-mile mark Bikila had caught up with the two men. These three ran together for about half an hour, during which time Bikila's teammates were not faring so well. Demissie Wolde was far back in the pack, and Mamo Wolde had dropped out altogether. Around the nine-mile mark, Bikila began to force the pace. The course was an out-and-back affair, and at the turnaround point Bikila led by five seconds over Hogan, with Clarke having fallen well behind. For Bikila, no more strategy was necessary. He slowly increased his lead, running with total concentration and precision—the ultimate image of the perfect marathoner. There was no indication that either his surgery or the extreme humidity was having the slightest effect on his race. His body seemed to float down the streets. Niskanen had taught him how to run using the least amount of energy and Bikila's smooth strides and motionless head made the race appear effortless. By the twenty-one mile mark, Bikila led by two and a half minutes, and Hogan was faltering. The Irishman slowed to a walk and eventually dropped out of the race, ceding second place to Tsuburaya.

Meanwhile, Bikila dashed on toward the finish, entering the stadium alone to the cheering of 70,000 spectators who watched history made as the Ethiopian became the first man to win two Olympic marathons. Bikila's time was a new world record of 2:12:11, more than a minute and a half faster than Heatley's previous mark, yet in spite of his incredible performance, he appeared fresh and rested at the end of the race. After crossing the finish line, he began a series of calisthenics in the infield—exercises designed to keep his body from stiffening after the race. The ease with which he performed stretches and bicycling exercises amazed the crowd. Later he told reporters that he could have maintained his pace for another six miles.

Following the race, Bikila expressed his eagerness to compete four years later in Mexico City where the altitude would be even higher than Addis Ababa, giving the Ethiopians a distinct advantage. Bikila vowed to do even better in 1968 than he had done in Tokyo.

The crowd that had so enthusiastically greeted Bikila had to wait several minutes before the second runner entered the stadium, but they erupted in cheers when they saw that he was their countryman Tsuburaya. Their enthusiasm was short lived this time, however, for Tsuburaya was followed by Basil Heatley of Great Britain just ten yards behind. Tsuburaya was clearly exhausted and Heatley passed him on the final curve to take the silver medal, finishing over four minutes behind Bikila. Still, Tsuburaya's bronze medal was the first for Japan in track and field in twenty-eight years, and he was hailed as a national hero. Later, when the medals were awarded, the band had to admit that it did not know the Ethiopian national anthem, so it took the opportunity to play the Japanese anthem instead.

Tsuburaya, a member of the Japanese Ground Self-Defence Force, soon discovered the stress that accompanied the role of national sports hero. Following the 1964 Games, he was forced to stop seeing his fiancée and begin full-time training for the 1968 marathon so that he might win the race for Japan. In 1967 he was hospitalized after two injuries. Though he recovered fully, he realized when he began training again that he would never be able to return to his previous level of competitiveness. On January 9, 1968, he committed suicide, leaving behind him a note that said simply, "Cannot run anymore."

Tsuburaya's story was a tragic reminder of the pressures of modern sport, and an illustration of why Pierre de Coubertin continually put forth his message that the glory of the Olympics is not in the victory but in the taking part.

17

The Games of the XIX Olympiad: Mexico City, 1968

The selection of Mexico City as the site of the 1968 Olympic Games had been met with something less than universal enthusiasm when it was announced in October of 1963. Critics claimed that the 7,347-foot altitude of the Mexican capital would pose a health risk to most athletes and provide an unfair advantage to those who hailed from similarly lofty regions. It would take more than such naysayers to quell the excitement of the Mexican sponsors, however. Unfortunately, many more storm clouds broke before the opening of the Games. Shortly before the close of the Winter Games in Grenoble in February, the IOC decided to re-admit South Africa to the Olympic family. Because of the policy of racial apartheid, South Africa had been excluded from the 1964 Games, but their decision to integrate their Olympic team swayed the IOC.

Immediately a storm of protest broke out. African nations announced they would boycott the Games and the Soviet Union and other countries joined the protest. Soon nearly forty countries were threatening to sit out the Games and the Mexicans were wondering if the opening day would ever come. Black athletes in the United States were also trying to organize a boycott, to protest the lack of civil rights for black citizens in their country. Three months later the IOC met again and reversed its decision on South Africa. A major boycott was averted, but racial issues still threatened the peace of the Games, especially as Americans were further enraged by the assassinations of Martin Luther King, Jr. and Robert Kennedy.

As the Games grew closer, however, trouble came from Mexico City itself. The unrest that had swept across U.S. college campuses during the previous year arrived in Mexico and the student area near the Olympic complex erupted in riots. Some students protested the vast sums spent on hosting the Olympics while poverty remained rampant in Mexico. The violence culminated on October 2, when police clashed with students and 260 people were killed. The Games were scheduled to open in eight days.

Despite all these problems, the Olympics opened on schedule. Far from hampering the athletes, the high altitude led to one world record after another on the track and in the field. The thin air was sliced through by sprinters, jumpers, and throwers. Twenty-six of the thirty track and field events were won with Olympic record or world record performances. The most dramatic of these was Bob Beamon's 29′ 2½″ leap in the long jump, which shattered the previous world record by nearly two feet. The Games did not totally escape the politics that had threatened them before the opening, though. Two black American athletes bowed their heads and raised their fists in a black power protest while standing on the medal platform during the playing of the national anthem.

The Mexico City marathon would be unique in the history of the Olympics. As in the track events, the altitude would have a tremendous effect on the race, but this time it would hinder rather than help the runners. Lung capacity would be as important as leg strength in this race, which would be run more than 1,000 feet higher than even Abebe Bikila's home course in Addis Ababa.

Bikila himself had been in and out of the running spotlight since his repeat win in Tokyo. He entered three marathons in 1965 and 1966, winning all three. When he arrived in Mexico City, however, he was training on an injured leg. He had dropped out of a race in July, but hoped that his experience with high altitude running might keep him in the Olympic competition. A week before the race he was diagnosed with a stress fracture in his foot and ordered by team officials not to compete, but he entered the race anyway.

Other favorites in the race included Derek Clayton of Australia, who had become the first man to run under 2:10 when he set a world record of 2:09:36 in Fukuoka, Japan in December of 1967. In 1969 in Antwerp, Clayton would run 2:08:33, setting a record that would stand for more than a decade. But in Mexico City he was worried. "There was a humidity problem," Clayton said later. "I have this allergy problem, which I tried to believe wasn't going to affect me, but after being there a while I knew it was going to be a problem."4

Naftali Temu of Kenya, who had won the gold medal in the 10,000 meters earlier in the Games also looked like a strong contender in the marathon, though in Tokyo he had finished only forty-ninth. Temu had come from five yards behind down the final stretch to beat Bikila's teammate Mamo Wolde for the gold. Wolde had originally planned to run the 5,000 meters and the marathon in addition to the 10,000 meters, but following his silver medal performance in the 10,000 meters, he developed an infected toe and withdrew from the other two races. The day before the marathon, though, Ethiopian officials asked him if he would enter the race, explaining that Bikila's injury might prevent him from finishing. Wolde agreed to run.

Wolde was far from unfamiliar with the Olympics. In the 1956 Games in Melbourne he had entered the 800 meters and 1,500 meters, in both cases finishing last in his qualifying heat. In the same Games, he ran the third leg for the Ethiopian 4×400 meters team. They, too, finished last in their heat. He did not participate in the 1960 Games, but he did travel to Rome to watch his close friend Abebe Bikila run the marathon. Wolde entered the 10,000 meters and the marathon in Tokyo in 1964. He finished in fourth place in the 10,000 meters, but was forced to drop out of the marathon. After losing the gold medal to Temu by such a small margin in the 10,000 meters, Wolde welcomed the chance for revenge. And, like Bikila, he hoped his high altitude experience would pay off in Mexico City. Toeing the line of the marathon start in 1968, Wolde looked back on an Olympic career of twelve years that covered races from 400 meters to the marathon. Though in peak condition, he had run an intensely competitive high-altitude 10,000 meters just a few days earlier. Now, at age thirty-five and running with an infected toe, did he have a chance to do the one thing he had never done in Olympic competition—win a gold medal?

The marathon was held on October 20 and featured a record seventy-four runners from forty-one countries. The course started in downtown Mexico City and made its way to the Olympic Stadium in the southern suburbs. For the first few miles, the lead pack included Bikila, Tim Johnston of Great Britain, Kenny Moore of the United States, and Nedo Farcic of Yugoslavia. By the nine-mile mark, Farcic and Johnston had opened up a slight lead. Just over a mile later, Bikila dropped out of the race. His injury had become too painful. Even the great Abebe Bikila could not run a marathon on a broken bone.

At the twelve-mile mark, Wolde received the news that Bikila had dropped out. Knowing now that only he could retain the marathon title for Ethiopia, he began to press the pace. By the fifteen-mile mark, Wolde and Temu, his nemesis from the 10,000 meters, had moved into the lead. Three miles later, Wolde surged ahead and thereafter was never threatened. If Bikila could not win the marathon for Ethiopia, Wolde would, and when he crossed the line in a respectable high-altitude time of 2:20:26, Ethiopian runners had won three Olympic marathons in a row, a feat never equalled before or since. Like many marathon victors, Wolde looked refreshed and happy at the end of the race. As he began his victory lap, a fan threw a straw hat to him and he broke into a smile, waving the hat at the cheering crowd and then placing it on his head as he jogged around the track.

With favorite runners such as Clayton and Temu suffering from the altitude, lesser known runners moved up through the field behind Wolde. Japanese who mourned the tragic death of Kokichi Tsuburaya took some comfort in the silver medal performance of Kenji Kimihara. Third place went to Mike Ryan of New Zealand. World record holder Derek Clayton finished seventh. American Kenny Moore came in fourteenth. Temu finished nineteenth. Once again, the Olympic Marathon had proven its unpredictability and its ability to slay giants.

One hour and fifteen minutes after Wolde won the 1968 marathon, with the stadium nearly empty, John Stephen Akhwari of Tanzania hobbled towards the finish line. In spite of a large bandage on his bloodied right leg, he refused to drop out of the race. By the time he passed through the tunnel into the stadium, he had slowed to a walk, but the few remaining spectators in the stands, as well as the volunteers along the track and in the infield cheered this final finisher as loudly as they had Wolde. Akhwari jogged around the track in pain and finally did what he had come to Mexico City to do—he crossed the finish line. Later he said that his people had not sent him to the Olympic Games to start a race; they had sent him to finish. Akhwari had truly been able to find the glory in participation, and his courage was applauded by all who watched.

Mamo Wolde said after the Mexico City race that if his teammate Abebe Bikila had not been injured he would have won the race, but Bikila never ran another marathon. Still, he was as loved as ever in his homeland. Haile Selassie promoted him to captain. The following year, while driving a Volkswagen that had been a gift from Emperor Selassie, Bikila collided with another car. He was paralyzed from the waist down. Bikila called his accident the "will of God." Haile Selassie sent Bikila to England for medical treatment, but there was no hope of restoring his world famous legs. When he returned to Ethiopia, carried off the plane on a stretcher, huge crowds welcomed him. Bikila became involved in paraplegic sports, particularly archery, but he would never walk or run again. The Munich Olympic Organizing Committee invited Bikila to the 1972 Games as an honored guest. There, he sat in his wheelchair and watched Frank Shorter win the marathon. After being presented with his gold medal, Shorter went first to Bikila to shake his hand.

On October 25, 1973, Bikila suffered a brain hemorrhage and died at the age of forty-one, leaving a wife and four children. He had run fifteen marathons in his career. He failed to finish two. Of the other thirteen, he won twelve. He had become as great a hero in Ethiopia as Spiridon Louis had in Greece so many decades before. Following his death, the Emperor proclaimed a national day of mourning. Sixty-five thousand people attended his funeral.

18

The Games of the XX Olympiad: Munich, 1972

With the staging of the 1972 Summer Olympics in Munich, West German officials hoped to erase the memory of the "Hitler Games" in 1936. A splendid Olympic complex was built and ceremonies were planned which were tastefully understated, in contrast to the overblown pomp of 1936. West Germany spent $600 million on Olympic preparations. As in 1968, racial unrest threatened the Games before they even started. This time the furor was over the IOC's decision to invite Rhodesia to the Games. Once again, the threat of the boycott by African nations and others forced the IOC to reconsider and the invitation was withdrawn.

On opening day, August 26, a record 7,830 athletes from a record 122 countries marched into the Olympic Stadium. When a young West German carried the Olympic torch on its final circuit of the track, he was accompanied by a sort of honor guard of distance runners from four continents— marathoners Derek Clayton of Australia and Kenji Kimihara of Japan as well as America's Jim Ryun and Kenyan Kip Keino.

In the first week of competition the spotlight was stolen by American swimmer Mark Spitz. In Mexico City, Spitz had failed to live up to predictions that he might win six gold medals, but he more than made up for that shortfall by winning seven golds in Munich.

On the track, surprises abounded, some as a result of foolish mistakes. Two Americans missed their heat in the 100 meters when their coach misread the schedule. Jim Ryun fell in his qualifying heat of the 1,500 meters and had to watch the finals from the sidelines. In the distance races, another "Flying Finn" seemed in the making. After dominating the distance races from 1912 to 1936, the Finns had not won a single gold medal in those events. Lasse Viren, a twenty-three-year-old with a sculpted face and a full beard, changed all that when he won gold in the 10,000 meters. He won the race and set a new world record despite a fall partway through the race. Viren added to his glory by taking the 5,000 meter gold a few days later. Unlike Emil Zátopek, though, Viren did not use his double victory as a springboard to running the marathon. At least not yet.

The eleventh day of the Games, September 5, brought a lull in the competition, and on that day a tragedy struck that would eclipse all the triumph of Munich and tarnish the Olympic movement forever. Eight armed Arab terrorists broke into the athletes' village and took nine Israelis hostage, killing two others. For the next day the world watched as ultimatums were given and West German negotiators attempted to avert a catastrophe. But the following morning, the news came. After transferring the terrorists and hostages to an airfield by helicopter, the police attacked. In the ensuing shoot-out all the hostages, five terrorists, and a West German policeman were killed. The Games were suspended for twenty-four hours and a memorial service was held in the Olympic Stadium. The Games would continue, but with a dark shadow cast over the previously joyful competitions.

The 1972 marathon field was crowded with possible medalists. Defending champion Mamo Wolde of Ethiopia was joined by his countryman Yetneberk Belete whom some were calling another Bikila. World record holder Derek Clayton and 1968 silver medalist Kenji Kimihara posed substantial threats as did Karel Lismont of Belgium who had won the European Championships in 1971. Ron Hill of England, who had run under 2:10 in winning the Commonwealth Championships in 1970 was considered by many the pre-race favorite. Also in the field was an American named Frank Shorter, who some pundits picked as a possible dark horse in the race. In no one's mind, however, was he a favorite.

Shorter was born in the town in which he was about to race, Munich, on October 31, 1947. His father had been stationed there following World War II, but very soon thereafter the family, which eventually numbered ten children, moved home to the United States, settling in Middletown, New York. In Mt. Hermon prep school, Shorter's running was primarily confined to a "Pie Race," a four and a half mile affair in which students competed for apple pies. He placed seventh in his first attempt, though in 1979 he returned to the school and ran the race for fun, setting a course record of 20:54, which still stands.

At Yale, Shorter ran on the track team, but did not take running too seriously. He missed spring training in the South so he could tour with a college singing group, and he was as likely to be found skiing as running. All that changed his senior year when his coach told him that, with work, he could make the Olympic marathon team. Shorter began to train seriously. In his senior year at Yale he was undefeated in dual meets in cross-country and he won the six-mile race in the NCAA Championships and finished second in the three-mile race.

For the next two years, Shorter led something of a nomadic existence, not sure exactly what he wanted to do with his life besides run, and always trying to stay one step ahead of the draft board. He almost enlisted in the Army to run on their track team, but opted out at the last minute. He participated in track meets from time to time. Eventually he enrolled in the University of Florida Law School and began to train even more intensely than he had previously. In June of 1971 he qualified for the Pan American Games marathon team, finishing second in the trials in a time of 2:17:44. He had attempted the distance only once before, dropping out of the Olympic trials in 1968. Thriving on the heat and humidity, Shorter won both the 10,000 meters and the marathon at the Pan American Games, and then set his sites on Munich. In late 1971, he ran the Fukuoka Marathon, winning and lowering his personal best time to 2:12:50. In the Olympic trial race, Shorter tied for first place with Kenny Moore. But Shorter did not win all his races leading up to the Olympic Marathon. A few days before the race he had placed fifth in the Olympic 10,000 meters race, setting an American record in the process. Now, at the start of the marathon, he faced the most prestigious field of runners he had ever seen.

As it had so often before, the race would start and finish in the Olympic Stadium. The course had been criticized in some quarters because of a plethora of tight corners and uneven road surfaces. Sixty-nine competitors from thirty-five nations left the starting line for two laps around the track. After the horror of the terrorist attack at the Olympic village, many of the runners were nervous about running for over two hours in the open streets. The British team had received death threats from the IRA, and no one felt immune to the possibility of more violence. Still, the runners remained in Munich and competed in the marathon. Shorter led the first lap around the track before being passed by another runner. After passing through the tunnel and out of the stadium, Shorter met with trouble.

"We left the street to get on a little path," said Shorter later. "At this point the camera truck had slowed down and all the runners were accordioned behind it, having to slow down. I tried to go to the right as everyone else was going to the left, because, since they were making a right hand turn, I figured I'd cut it close and save some distance. Well, the truck decided he'd pull off the road at this point. So here I was running along with the driver pushing me off the road, pinching me between the side of the truck and the crowd. I knew I wasn't going to get by, so I pounded on the truck, swore a few times, and then stopped and went around the back. I hit it with my hand, so at that point everyone assumed that I'd been struck. I lost twenty or thirty yards on that little caper."[5]

Shorter was not the only American to experience problems in the early going. His teammate Kenny Moore was caught between other runners on a tight corner and tripped. By the time he could get back on his feet in the crowd of runners he had lost thirty yards and his elbow and knee stung where they had scraped the asphalt.

The race continued at a fairly comfortable pace, with Shorter staying in the lead pack. At the six-mile mark, the painted blue line that the runners were following turned into the first of the two parks the course would pass through—Nymphenburg. In Nymphenburg and in the next park, The English Garden, the course would cover eight miles of loose gravel and dirt. IAAF regulations required that the marathon be run on pavement, so the Munich Organizing Committee agreed to sweep the paths through the park free of loose material and cover them with a special plastic. As soon as the runners turned into Nymphenburg they realized that this promise had not been kept. Thick dust from the press bus billowed in front of the runners. Though the bus eventually turned aside and the air cleared, the runners now knew that the uneven surfaces in the two parks would have to be taken into account in their race strategies.

At the first refreshment station an Ethiopian runner, Lengisse Bedane, took the bottle of flat Coke that Frank Shorter had prepared for himself. Shorter instinctively grabbed Kenny Moore's bottle. As the two teammates ran through the park, Shorter apologized. The rules were different at that time. He could not give Moore the bottle because rules forbade competitors from helping each other. So, Moore went without refreshment through the early miles of the race.

As the miles clicked by, each of the runners watched the others to see when a break would come. By the time the runners emerged from the park back onto the pavement, the lead pack was down to eight. World record holder Derek Clayton and Englishman Ron Hill, who had pushed the early pace, had fallen behind. The remaining runners wondered who would force the pace. Who would be left behind? Perhaps because of this paranoia, the pace began to slow, and Shorter felt uncomfortable. His running rhythm was based on a faster pace. Finally, before the nine-mile mark, Shorter relaxed and let his own rhythm determine his pace. Almost before he knew it he was ten yards in front of the pack. No one followed him—all, perhaps, thinking it was too soon to make a break. Surely Shorter would return to the pack.

But Shorter kept up his pace, opening up a larger and larger lead. Behind him the pack was falling apart. Kenny Moore and a revived Derek Clayton began to work their way through the other runners, including Karel Lismont of Belgium and defending champion Mamo Wolde. Wolde joined with Moore and Clayton in the chase, but by the halfway mark in the race, Shorter's lead was over one minute. At the fifteen-mile mark, Clayton slowed for too long at a water stop and Moore and Wolde were alone, apparently battling for the silver.

With nine miles to go, the race entered the second park, The English Garden. Shorter had to slow his pace somewhat to avoid slipping on the gravel, but the runners behind him would have to slow as well. Kenny Moore even had to hurdle a small dog who had run out onto the course, but he and Wolde continued to run together. Behind them, Clayton had disappeared and barely visible was Karel Lismont, the European champion.

With five miles to go, Moore was stricken by a sudden cramp in his right hamstring. Wolde passed him immediately as he hobbled in pain. Forced to slow down and work through his cramp, Moore was soon passed by Lismont as well. His battle for the silver medal had suddenly turned into a fight to finish the race.

Meanwhile, with three miles left, Shorter's lead was two minutes. The hundreds of thousands of spectators who lined the streets of Munich and the millions who watched the first marathon to be televised live from start to finish began to realize that Frank Shorter was about to win America's first gold medal in the event in sixty-four years.

When he entered the stadium, Shorter was within easy striking distance of Abebe Bikila's Olympic Marathon record, and he emerged from the tunnel into the bright light of the arena expecting to hear a roar of cheering erupt from the crowd. What he heard, however, was a chorus of boos and jeers. Shorter was nonplussed, but he continued his progress around the track. Unbeknownst to him, a German student named Norbert Sudhaus, had dodged the tight security and run into the stadium just in front of Shorter. For a moment, many in the crowd believed that he was the leader of the marathon. Sudhaus had run a full lap around the track before security guards grabbed him and ushered him out of the arena. The cries of contempt that Shorter heard were aimed at Sudhaus, not him.

Only one question remained about Shorter's certain victory. Would he break Bikila's Olympic record? Shorter clearly had a reserve of energy. A quick sprint around the track would bring him not only a gold medal but an Olympic record. But Shorter did not sprint. He finished the race at the same pace he had been running for many miles. "I've always maintained that anyone who's leading by any significant amount at the end of a marathon who sprints at the end is hot-dogging," Shorter said.

Shorter's winning time was 2:12:19, seven seconds shy of Bikila's record. He may have had another reason for steering clear of the record. Bikila, now paralyzed and in a wheelchair, was in the stands watching the finish. Any marathoner might have done what Shorter did and let the record stand out of respect for the great Abebe Bikila.

Karel Lismont of Belgium, who had been previously undefeated at the marathon distance, passed Wolde in the final miles and took the silver medal in Munich. Defending champion Mamo Wolde, at the age of forty, became the oldest runner to win an Olympic Marathon medal, capping a sixteen-year Olympic career with a bronze. In spite of his leg cramp, Kenny Moore took fourth place, making it a most successful day for the American team. Derek Clayton, however, who loved to run in cool weather, found himself looking for liquid at every aid station. He could not perform well in the hot, humid weather and faded in the later miles, finishing in thirteenth place.

Mamo Wolde, owner of gold and bronze medals in the Olympic Marathon, a national hero in his homeland, and one of the most versatile and enduring runners in Olympic history, was arrested in 1992 as part of an attempt by the new Ethiopian government to punish the human rights abuses of the communist regime, which ruled there for seventeen years. But Wolde has never been officially charged with any crime. In spite of attempts at intervention by Amnesty International, the IOC, and the IAAF, he remains in prison. In a remarkable show of Olympic brotherhood, Kenny Moore, who became a journalist after his running career, visited Wolde in prison in 1995. Moore endured several hours of imprisonment himself before he was able to convince Ethiopian officials to let him see Wolde. He knew his fellow Olympian only from the few words they had spoken on the streets of Munich—in Mexico City, Moore had been too far behind to speak to Wolde. But when Wolde saw Moore for less than ten minutes in a prison in Addis Ababa, he embraced him warmly.

"It all comes back," he said. "I remember you had a goatee. Thank you, thank you from my family for this. Remember me to the brothers, the Olympic brothers."

When Moore told Wolde of all those in the Olympic movement who did remember Wolde and who had sent their best wishes, Wolde replied, "These are words from God."[6]

Frank Shorter became the first American in sixty-four years to win the Olympic Marathon, but in many ways he can be considered the first real American gold medalist in the event. After all, Thomas Hicks, who won in 1904, was given drugs to help him stay upright and was even physically assisted in the late stages of the race. Johnny Hayes won in 1908 only because of the disqualification of Dorando Pietri. Shorter had more than earned his gold medal, running in front and alone for much of the day and proving that the dark horse doesn't always come from behind to win.

19

The Games of the XXI Olympiad: Montreal, 1976

Following the tragic events of Munich, the Olympic movement badly needed to reassert itself at the Montreal Games. The city went into major debt to try to assure that the Games of 1976 would brighten the tarnished image of the Olympics; $1.2 billion was spent on the Games, including $100 million for security and $650 million for a new Olympic stadium.

All appeared to be in readiness for a controversy-free Olympics until forty-eight hours before the Games when the racial tensions that had threatened the past two Olympics finally erupted. This time the complaint was against New Zealand, which had sent a rugby team to compete in South Africa. A group of African and Caribbean nations complained that this violated the ban on competition with the apartheid state of South Africa and that New Zealand should be banned from the Games. With the Opening Ceremonies only two days away, nearly thirty countries, about a fourth of the total invited, packed their bags and headed home. It was the first major boycott in Olympic history. Unfortunately it would not be the last.

The Games opened without the boycotting nations on July 17, and in the pomp, ceremony, and excitement of the Olympic pageant, much of the controversy of the preceding days was forgotten. There were still over six thousand athletes from ninety-two nations competing for Olympic glory.

Every Olympic Games has its unexpected heroes, and Montreal was no exception. In this case the athlete of the hour was a four-foot eleven-inch, fourteen-year-old Romanian gymnast named Nadia Comaneci. As television commentators struggled to pronounce her name, Comaneci won three gold medals and the hearts of the world. Not only did she score the first perfect ten ever given in international competition, she added six more perfect tens before the competition was over.

Lasse Viren of Finland once again dominated the long-distance events on the track, winning the 5,000 and 10,000 meters and thus becoming the first Olympian to pull off that impressive double in two Olympics. This time, however, Viren decided he would attempt to follow in the footsteps of Emil Zátopek, and announced that he would enter the marathon.

Though Frank Shorter had run the 1972 marathon as a relative unknown, he stepped to the starting line in Montreal as an international celebrity and a favorite to win the race. In the intervening four years he had won six of the eight marathons he had entered, all but one of those wins coming in times faster than his gold medal performance of 1972. Shorter's victory in the Munich marathon had touched off a running boom in the United States, and while that boom was still in its infancy, millions of Americans tuned in to watch Shorter defend his title. Following 1976, millions of Americans would take to the roads inspired by the success of Shorter. But Shorter had also been suffering from a hairline ankle fracture, which sometimes made it difficult for him to maintain consistently hard training. If the race came down to a battle in the final miles, that might cause a problem.

Another American hope in the Montreal race had been Bill Rodgers, who placed second in the Olympic trials by only seven seconds and who had won the Boston Marathon in 1975 in a time of 2:09:55. Though Rodgers was to be one of the most consistently successful marathoners of the next decade, he entered the Olympics with a foot injury, and finished fortieth in a time of 2:25:14.

Lasse Viren was a wild card in the marathon. Like Zátopek, he had never run the distance before entering the Olympics, and he had won the gold medal in the 5,000 meters just a day before the marathon. Yet his incredible success on the track made him popular with the crowd. Like Zátopek in 1952, he seemed invincible.

Karel Lismont of Belgium, the silver medal winner in 1972, also returned for the 1976 Games, and Jerome Drayton of Canada was certainly the favorite of the cheering crowds that lined the marathon route.

July 31 brought muggy weather to Montreal, as marathon day had to so many other Olympic cities. Sixty-seven competitors from thirty-five nations lined up for the start of the race. Despite the boycott, the field was almost exactly the same size as four years earlier.

Bravely withstanding the pain of his foot injury, Bill Rodgers led the race for the first six miles, taking two other runners with him out in front of the large lead pack. He had some hope that a fast early pace might tire out Viren, whose entry Rodgers resented as an insult to marathon specialists. By the nine-mile mark, Rodgers had dropped back and the lead pack still consisted of twelve runners. Three miles later it had whittled down to eight as Frank Shorter began to push the pace. But the real race began just past the halfway mark. Rain had begun to fall on the runners, and defending champion Shorter decided it was time to make his move. He surged ahead, leaving the lead pack behind. At first the inexperienced Viren tried to keep up with Shorter, but within a few hundred yards he had given up and returned to the pack. The last ten miles of the race loomed ahead as a possible repeat of 1972.

Four minutes later that possibility evaporated as Waldemar Cierpinski of East Germany pulled up on Shorter's shoulder and began running with him stride for stride. Cierpinski was unknown to Shorter as he was to most of the rest of the field and the spectators. He had been trained by the East German sports system, a system that put children in special sports schools as early as age eight and used a vast array of publicly funded scientists, trainers, and facilities to try to form champions. Cierpinski, who grew up in a farming village near Halle, first competed in athletics in school at age seven. He favored boxing, but eventually turned to running.

He entered the sports system at the age of twelve, when he showed a talent for cross-country running. He was trained first at Aufbau Nienburg, a factory sports club, and later was sent to a special boarding school in Halle. At sixteen he was entered in the annual Spartakiad, a massive sports festival for East German youth. For seven years he was trained by the East German system. There was only one problem. The system was training him to compete in the 3,000 meter steeplechase.

"The tempo over the 3,000 meter distance was simply too fast for me," he said later. "Training for it certainly promoted the development of my basic speed, but the marathon distance was more my cup of tea."[7]

Cierpinski watched Frank Shorter win the 1972 marathon in Munich and immediately became interested in marathoning. He entered his first marathon on a lark, while vacationing in Czechoslovakia in 1974, placing third with a time of 2:20:20 in poor running conditions. Among those he defeated was British star Ron Hill. The next year he ran the same marathon again, finishing seventh, but improving his time to 2:17:30. In 1976 he had run two marathons—the Karl Marx Stadt in April, which he won in a time of 2:13:57, and the East German Olympic trial in May, which he won in 2:12:21.

Cierpinski's marathoning prowess apparently convinced the East German officials that this was indeed his true distance and that he had a chance to strike gold in Montreal. He was sent to the Games as the only member of the East German marathon team. He had studied all of Frank Shorter's races and followed all of Shorter's training methods, yet he still expected to finish no better than tenth. His secret hope was to somehow win a bronze medal. Now, with ten miles to go in the Olympic Marathon, he was running even with the defending champion.

"It was a wonderful feeling when I came alongside," Cierpinski said. "I glanced at Shorter as I did so, and looked right into the eyes of the man who was my idol as a marathon runner. I knew all about him. And yet I could tell by the return glance that he didn't know much, if anything, about me. The psychological advantage was mine."

It was true that Shorter knew nothing about his challenger. Cierpinski was not wearing the standard East German blue uniform, but a plain white top, which he had chosen to reflect the heat of the sun—an ironic choice given the rainy weather. Shorter later admitted that he thought his competitor was Carlos Lopes of Portugal.

Frank Shorter ran in surges, and as the two battled each other through the next several miles, Cierpinski answered each surge Shorter made. "Each surge he made had less distance and was run with less strength," said Cierpinski. "They became easier to make up. As the race went on, I started to gain confidence." Cierpinski was surprised at how good he felt running in the cooling rain.

Finally, Cierpinski put on a surge of his own and broke into the lead. By the twenty-one mile mark he led by two hundred yards over Shorter. But Shorter was not about to give up his chance to repeat as gold medalist. He put on another surge and by twenty-four miles he had cut Cierpinski's lead to a mere twenty yards. But Cierpinski surged once more, and this time, the race was over. By the twenty-five mile mark, Cierpinski's lead over Shorter was thirty-two seconds. As he approached the stadium the East German national anthem was being played inside as part of the award ceremony for the women's 4 × 400 meter relay race, which had been won by the East German team. But Cierpinski couldn't hear the music because of the encouraging shouts of the crowd that lined the street.

Cierpinski surged into the stadium, winning the race in a time of 2:09:55, becoming the first man to run the Olympic Marathon in under 2:10. After crossing the line, though, Cierpinski kept running. He had become confused after taking his final lap around the track when he looked up and saw the "one lap to go" sign being held by an official. Shorter had entered the stadium, and the sign was being displayed for him, but Cierpinski was not about to take any chances, so he kept running for one more lap. When he crossed the line a second time, silver medalist Shorter was waiting there to congratulate him on his victory. Shorter had run one of the fastest races of his career, finishing at 2:10:45, and could hardly be too disappointed in his silver.

Behind the two leaders the pack had finally dissolved and the race for the bronze was on. Drayton of Canada, Viren, and Lismont, were running about fifty seconds behind Shorter, but American Don Kardong was moving up fast. With just over a mile to go, Kardong moved into third, with Lismont trailing him by less than a stride. Inside the stadium, though, Kardong, who was suffering leg cramps, could not hold off a charge from the Belgian, and Lismont added a bronze medal to the silver he had won in 1972. Kardong, finishing in fourth place, still broke Abebe Bikila's Olympic record. Lasse Viren, whose entry had surprised so many, finished a respectable fifth, running 2:13:10 in his first marathon. Twenty seconds behind him came Canadian Jerome Drayton, who earned the cheers of his countrymen.

With Americans finishing second and fourth, the 1976 marathon solidified the new found presence of the United States in marathon running. Bill Rodgers was just beginning the most successful years of his career, and he and other American marathoners looked forward to Moscow as another opportunity to ride the crest of the running wave that now swept across America.

As for Cierpinski, the years between Olympics were not his best. He suffered a series of injuries, and during the late 1970s was not able to run within five minutes of his gold medal winning time in Montreal. Pundits dismissed him as a one race wonder, but he, like everyone else, waited for Moscow.

20

The Games of the XXII Olympiad: Moscow, 1980

The most significant event of the Moscow Olympic Games took place over six months before the Opening Ceremonies when Soviet tanks rolled into Afghanistan on December 28, 1979. The invasion came ostensibly at the request of the Afghan leadership, but that leadership had been installed the day before by the Soviets. The world was outraged, and none more than American President Jimmy Carter. With the Moscow Olympics only months away, Carter announced that the U.S. team would boycott the Games and he encouraged other freedom-loving countries to do the same. Sixty-one countries did just that, making the boycott of 1980 the largest in Olympic history.

Of the eighty-one nations who did send athletes, many allowed individuals to decide for themselves whether to attend, so the ranks of world class competitors were further depleted by those who chose to protest on their own.

The Soviets seemed unfazed by the protest, and certainly realized the terrific propaganda potential of even a boycotted Olympics. Eager to show that the Soviet state was efficient and successful, they spent an unprecedented $9 billion in preparation for the Games. Though the pageantry was unmatched, in much of the world the Moscow Games passed with as little notice as any ordinary international track meet. Sixteen of the eighty-one teams that participated refused to parade their national flags in the Opening Ceremonies in support of the boycotting nations. Soviet television cameras deftly skipped over the protestors.

The Soviets had wanted to stage an Olympics that would call attention to their politics, but little did they suspect that politics would so totally dominate these Games. The innocence that had been lost in Munich seemed to disappear altogether in Moscow. Not only did political conflicts fail to stop for the Olympics, but the Olympics became wrapped up in those conflicts to their own permanent damage.

The list of runners absent at the start of the marathon included Bill Rodgers, who had run sixteen marathons since Montreal and won thirteen of them, including recording a time of 2:09:27 in the 1979 Boston Marathon. Toshihiko Seko may have been the best chance Japan had had for Olympic Marathon gold since the country usurped the services of Sohn Kee Chung in 1936. In the eighteen months before the Games, Seko had run three marathons in under 2:11.

In spite of the absences, the field in the 1980 race was still impressive. Soviet record holder Vladimir Kotov, who had run 2:10:58 in May, represented the best hopes of the home crowd to bring glory to their nation. Waldemar Cierpinski had broken out of a rut of slow times and disappointing finishes with a 2:11:17 in a marathon in May. Lasse Viren, who placed fifth in the 10,000 meters in his third Olympics, was again giving the marathon distance a try. Gerard Nijboer of Holland had shocked the running world when he turned in a time of 2:09:01, a European record, in a race in Amsterdam in April. Not surprisingly, the field was rounded out with other top Soviet athletes. The Japanese and Americans would be missed, but it still promised to be quite a race.

Ironically, forty nations, more than ever before, were represented by the seventy-four runners in the Moscow marathon. The course led out of the Olympic stadium and along the banks of the Moscow River, and it was the Soviet champion Kotov who led the early stages of the race, holding onto the lead through the half-way point. The first to challenge Kotov for the lead was Lasse Viren, but he was stricken with an attack of diarrhea and forced to drop out of the race. Next to break for the lead was Rodolfo Gomez of Mexico. He led for several miles, until the real race began at about the twenty-two mile mark.

At that point, Cierpinski, Nijboer, and a pair of Soviet runners, Leonid Moseyev and Satymkul Dzumanazarov, overtook Gomez and the battle for the gold was on. Nijboer was famous for his blistering speed in the final miles of a marathon, but when he moved into the lead, Cierpinski was ready, just as he had been in Montreal four years earlier. Cierpinski caught Nijboer, then put on a surge of his own and passed the Dutchman to become the second person in history to win two Olympic marathons. Cierpinski's time was 2:11:02, his second best ever. Only his winning performance in Montreal had been faster.

Behind Cierpinski, the evenness of the field was demonstrated. As he approached the finish line, five runners circled the track at once, an Olympic record. Nijboer held on for the silver medal, finishing just seventeen seconds behind Cierpinski, and Dzumanazarov gave the bronze medal to the home team.

What would have happened in the 1980 marathon without the boycott? It is difficult to say. Certainly the field that ran was a fine and competitive one, with seven runners finishing under the 2:13 mark. True, the winning times in two of the three other major international marathons that year (New York and Fukuoka) were faster than the Olympic winning time, but comparing performances in one marathon with another is futile, because times in the race depend so much on weather, the difficulty of the course, and psychological factors.

Though Waldemar Cierpinski may never be considered quite the equal of Abebe Bikila because of the shadow cast on the Moscow Olympics by the boycott, he nonetheless rests securely in the pantheon of great marathoners. And if Cierpinski was the beneficiary of a boycott in 1980, he would be the victim of one in 1984. The era of the boycotted Olympics had not yet ended.

21

The Games of the XXIII Olympiad: Los Angeles, 1984

In 1984, the Summer Olympics returned to American soil after fifty-two years and took up residence not only in the same city, but in the very stadium they had occupied in 1932. Although that stadium was only one of twenty-three Olympic sites scattered across southern California, it would serve as the setting for the Hollywood style Opening and Closing Ceremonies and the finish for the men's and, for the first time ever, women's marathons.

The Los Angeles Games were organized by a committee headed by businessman Peter Uberroth, who managed to turn the elaborate and far-flung spectacle into a money-making event, in spite of the fact that no local taxes were allocated for the Games. With American television prepared to beam live events into the homes of millions during prime time and with all the entertainment wizardry of California thrown behind the presentation of the Games, they looked to be the biggest and most glamorous ever.

Though some feared that the Soviet Union might boycott the Games in retaliation for the American led boycott of the Moscow Games, by late spring that threat seemed to have passed. Then, on May 8, 1984, the Russian National Olympic Committee issued a statement claiming that extremist groups in America were planning to make conditions unbearable for Soviet athletes and that American organizers were not planning to provide the Soviet team with sufficient security. For these reasons, the statement said, the Soviet athletes would not be able to compete in the Games. The claims made in the statement about protests and security seemed entirely fabricated, given the facts, and most viewed the Soviet boycott as simple tit-for-tat. Thirteen Soviet Bloc nations joined the boycott, but in spite of this, athletes from 140 nations marched into the Los Angeles Coliseum on July 28, the most countries ever represented at an Olympic Games. Even China had returned to the Olympic family for the first time since 1952.

With competition lacking from the Soviet Union, East Germany, and other athletically powerful eastern European countries, the teams from the United States rolled to victory in a fashion that had to make even the staunchest patriot somewhat embarrassed. Heroes and heroines were born overnight. Mary Lou Retton became the first American woman to win the gold in all-around gymnastics and was appearing in television commercials within months. Greg Louganis won gold in both the springboard and platform diving competition. Carl Lewis repeated the feat of the great Jesse Owens, becoming the first man since 1936 to win four gold medals in track and field in a single Olympics. In all, the Americans won 83 of the 223 gold medals awarded in Los Angeles.

The marathon was notable for the absence of the defending champion, Cierpinski, who was a victim of the boycott. But Cierpinski was now thirty-four years old, and had not run especially well in recent marathons. Still, pre-race pundits who made their prediction before the boycott was announced pointed to Cierpinski's 2:10:37 in the European Championships of 1983 as evidence that the mysterious runner who shows up every four years to collect his Olympic gold might have one more win left in him.

Despite Cierpinski's absence, the 1984 Olympic Marathon field may well have been the greatest yet assembled. Seven runners in the race had personal best times of under 2:09, fully a minute faster than the Olympic record. It was a race full of favorites, many of whom had been forced to sit out the 1980 race and were all the more eager for their shot at Olympic gold. Toshihiko Seko of Japan had entered five marathons since placing second at Boston in 1979 and won all five of them. Alberto Salazar of the United States won the first four marathons he entered, beginning with New York in 1980, where he ran the fastest first marathon ever, 2:09:41. The following year he predicted that he would break Derek Clayton's twelve-year-old world record at New York, and he did, running a 2:08:12.7 in his second marathon. 1982 brought wins at New York and Boston, both under 2:10. Salazar had struggled in the year leading up to the Olympics, however. He had also shown his susceptibility to heat when he collapsed with heat exhaustion in a race in 1978. With a starting time planned for 5:30 P.M. so the East Coast could watch the race in prime time, the Los Angeles marathon promised to be a warm affair.

If anyone was the favorite of the favorites in this race it was Robert de Castella of Australia. Not only was he the current world champion, with a personal best of 2:08:18, but he hailed from Sydney, where he trained in a climate similar to that in Los Angeles. Then there were the Africans, always unpredictable in an Olympic Marathon and certainly capable of dealing with heat. Juma Ikangaa of Tanzania and Joseph Nzau of Kenya might just make an impact on the race.

If some dismissed Cierpinski's absence as irrelevant because he had reached the ripe old age of thirty-four, they must certainly have given no chance to Portugal's Carlos Lopes. Lopes had competed in the Olympics in 1976, when Frank Shorter mistook Cierpinski for Lopes, but after eight years he was now thirty-seven—certainly too old to have much effect on the race, especially considering he was hit by a car while training just fifteen days before the marathon. He was lucky enough to escape with minor injuries, though, and still planned to compete. Lopes had only completed one marathon in his life, though this was a two-second loss to de Castella. Marathoning was like a second career for Lopes. He had won the world cross-country title in 1976 and again in 1984, before taking the silver medal behind Lasse Viren in the 10,000 meters in the Montreal Games. The 10,000 meters was still his speciality in 1984 when he pushed Fernando Mamede to a world record performance at that distance. As a marathoner, he was just beginning.

Runners and runners' groups had protested the starting time of the marathon as inhumane. No one would be foolish enough to run a marathon in Los Angeles in August, much less one that started in the late afternoon. But although the women's race, which was expected to draw less television interest, started at the relatively cool hour of 8:00 A.M., the men lined up for the start at Santa Monica College in the heat of late afternoon. Of course, most Olympic marathons have been run in heat, one reason they have so seldom resulted in world records, which are more often set in cooler seasons. With the threat of smog, the certainty of heat, and the hilly course that lay ahead of them, none of the men could have been planning for an Olympic record. They all just wanted to finish first.

When the starter's gun sounded, 107 men from sixty nations, by far the largest field in Olympic Marathon history, started around the track. The first half of the race, with the course winding along the Pacific coast, saw a large pack of leaders as expected. At the fifteen-mile mark, twelve men still ran in the lead pack, with the pace being set by Ikangaa. Runners dropped backed gradually, but the first surprise came when de Castella fell back at the twenty-mile mark. "I stopped to get a drink and when I looked up the leading guys had fifty meters on me," said the Australian. "Before I knew it it was 100. It was very hot, but I can't put it down to one or two things. I just on this day didn't have it."[8]

With six miles to go, seven men led the race. A mile later, Seko was the next casualty, dropping out of the lead pack and ultimately finishing fourteenth. Following the race he said he had been bothered by stomach problems since arriving in Los Angeles. Up to this point, about twenty-one miles into the marathon, it had been a race of attrition. Now the time had come for someone to make a move. That move came from an unexpected source, Charlie Spedding of Great Britain. Spedding had run only two marathons prior to Los Angeles, and though he had won them both he was not considered a threat to medal at the Olympics. But Spedding forced the pace, and only two other runners could stay with him—Carlos Lopes, the thirty-seven year old who was trying to finish his second marathon ever, and John Treacy of Ireland who had placed ninth in the 10,000 meters and was running in his first marathon ever. In a field a favorites, an upset was in the making.

Lopes did not wait long to challenge the other two runners. Less than a mile later, in the words of Treacy, "Lopes just took off. Charlie and I tried to go with him, but we just didn't have it. At that point I knew I was going for the silver." Lopes, in fact, ran the next three miles at an incredible 4:41 per mile. He breezed into the Olympic stadium alone, having defied the demons of age, heat, and injury. His winning time was as shocking as his victory—2:09:21, a new Olympic record. John Treacy hung on for the silver medal, followed two seconds later by Charlie Spedding who took bronze. The race that had been so eagerly anticipated turned out as no one could have guessed.

In spite of the fact that the favorites finished out of the medals (de Castella fifth, Ikangaa sixth, Seko fourteenth, Salazar fifteenth) the times showed how brilliant the performances in this race had been. The Soviets had bragged, and rightly so, that the first seven finishers in the 1980 race had all come in under 2:13. The 1984 marathon saw three runners finish under 2:10, and a time of 2:11:39 earned only eighth place.

The story of the 1984 Olympic Marathon is one of remarkable times and superb competition, but mention should be made of the last place finisher, Dieudonne Lamothe of Haiti. Haitian dictator "Baby Doc" Duvalier had taken to sending personal friends or acquaintances to compete in the Olympic Games, resulting in track races where Haitians finished several laps behind trained athletes from other nations. Lamothe had competed in 1976, recording the slowest time in Olympic history in the 5,000 meters. Though he made no public statements during the Games of 1984, he revealed after the fall of Duvalier that officials from Haiti had threatened to kill him if he failed to complete the marathon course. With a motivation unlike any of the other runners, Lamothe crossed the finish line in a time of 2:52:18. To his credit, after Duvalier was forced out of power, Lamothe improved his personal best to 2:26:23 in the New York Marathon, presumably under somewhat less pressure. But 1984 would not be Lamothe's final Olympics even if it was the last time he would be sent to the Games by a dictator.

Despite the Soviet led boycott and the absence of the defending champion, the 1984 Olympic Marathon had been one of the great races in the history of the event. Gold medal winner Carlos Lopes expressed the thoughts of many a racer when he said, "When I entered the stadium I felt very happy. I felt compensated for all the hard work." Lopes went on to set a world record of 2:07:12 in the marathon at the age of thirty-eight. In 1986, he retired from competitive running.

22

The Games of the XXIV Olympiad: Seoul, 1988

For sixteen years the Olympics had been plagued by politics and major boycotts. When the announcement was made that the 1988 Games would be held in Seoul, South Korea, fears of more political protests immediately broke out. After all, South Korea was still technically at war with its northern neighbor. North Korea was firmly allied with the Soviet Union, and as everyone had seen in 1984, the Soviet Union had the power to keep East Germany and other countries out of the Games. What could the IOC be thinking when they chose to award the Games to such a potentially volatile city?

In short, they were thinking that they had no choice. Only Nagoya, Japan had joined Seoul in bidding for the 1988 Games, and that city was deeply divided over the issue of hosting the Olympics, with petitions and protests being sent to the IOC begging that the Japanese city not be chosen.

But despite all their potential for trouble, the Seoul Olympics turned out to be the most peaceful in decades. Few countries joined North Korea's boycott, with the only significant athletic power being Cuba. Ethiopia did join, however, leaving the world record holder in the marathon, Belaine Densimo, who had run a blistering 2:06:50, at home. One hundred and sixty nations competed, twenty more than ever before. With 9,421 athletes competing in twenty-three sports, the Seoul Games were the biggest ever. The Soviet Union and East Germany both sent large and successful teams, never suspecting that this would be the last Olympics in which those countries would compete. By 1992, they would no longer exist.

The Opening Ceremonies were moving as always, but especially so for fans of the marathon race. When the torch entered the Olympic stadium and was carried around the track to light the Olympic flame, it was held by one of the great heroes of South Korean sport, Sohn Kee Chung, who had won the Olympic Marathon in 1936. Then, he had been forced to run under the flag of occupying Japan, but now, at age seventy-six, Sohn ran as a Korean, proudly holding aloft the Olympic torch while tens of thousands of his countrymen stood and cheered.

The running events are always the focus of much attention, but in 1988 they grabbed more headlines than ever. First Canada's Ben Johnson stunned the world by becoming the fastest human in history in the 100 meters. Then he stunned the world again by testing positive for performance enhancing steroids. His gold medal was taken away and given to second place finisher Carl Lewis. Florence Griffith-Joyner of the United States won three gold medals in the sprints, setting a world mark in the 200 meters.

All these events took place amidst the greatest security ever provided for an Olympic Games. Police and metal detectors abounded, but all proceeded peacefully, with the excitement of the Games building toward the traditional final event, the men's marathon. No event showed off the care the South Koreans had taken to ensure a safe Olympics better than the marathon, for the route was lined with fifty thousand policemen.

Despite the fact that the start of the Olympics was delayed until late September to provide for cooler weather, the marathon, as had become the tradition, was run in unpleasantly humid conditions. A record field of 118 racers represented sixty-six nations.

Several runners returned from the 1984 race to try to avenge their losses. Toshihiko Seko had continued his stellar career after Los Angeles. In the previous nine years of running marathons, the 1984 Olympic race was his only loss. Seko did not like racing in the heat, but was still picked as a favorite to win the race by some analysts. Bronze medalist Charlie Spedding was back as were Robert de Castella and Juma Ikangaa. But four years of marathon history had passed since 1984, and these veteran runners would face strong challenges, even with world record holder Densimo out of the race.

Many newcomers to world class marathoning figured to play a role in the Seoul race. Douglas Wakiihuri of Kenya had been a virtual unknown when he won the World Championships the previous year in Rome. Now he lived and trained with Toshihiko Seko and was considered a major threat. Seko's teammate Takeyuki Nakayama held the course record for the Seoul marathon course. Ahmed Saleh of Djibouti, had won the 1987 World Cup on the same course the Olympic race would be run on and had also run the second fastest marathon ever, 2:07:07, a few months before the Games. Italian Gelindo Bordin may have thought that history was on his side. After all, he, like 1984 winner Carlos Lopes, had been hit by a car. In Bordin's case, though, the accident, which had happened back in April of 1981, was more serious. Bordin had lain unconscious on the ground for six hours and had been presumed dead after being hit from behind during a training run in Verona.

The marathon was scheduled to start at 2:35 P.M., in the heat of the day. The Olympic planners seemed more concerned with finishing the race just before the Closing Ceremonies than with providing good running conditions for the competitors. The course was ideal for track runners as it would follow the Han River on flat, wide streets.

Despite rumors of a potential tear-gas attack on the runners, the race began as scheduled, starting much as the Los Angeles marathon had, with a large lead pack running together. Ikangaa set the pace, just as he had in 1984, and the early pace was blistering. When Charlie Spedding checked his watch and told Robert de Castella that the pace translated into 4:50 miles, de Castella said, "We're all going to die out here today."9

By the halfway point, the lead pack was down to fifteen runners. The heat was taking its toll on the field. The lead pack consisted primarily of runners from Japan, Australia, Kenya, and Mexico. Crashing this four-way party were Ahmed Saleh of Djbouti and Gelindo Bordin of Italy.

The race began in earnest at nineteen miles, when the lead pack was down to seven runners—Spedding, Seko, Saleh, Wakiihuri, Ikangaa, Bordin, and Nakayama.

The first surge came from Nakayama, with the result that Seko and Spedding were left behind. The lead pack was down to five and Seko, who was invincible outside the Olympics, had seen his chances for a medal in Seoul disappear. Spedding fought his way back to the lead pack but when the next surge came from Nakayama and Saleh just short of the twenty-two mile mark, Spedding and Ikangaa lost contact with the leaders for good. A mile later, Nakayama could no longer keep up the pace and he dropped back leaving Saleh, Wakiihuri, and Bordin to decide the medals. These three had also been the medalists at the World Championships the previous year, where Bordin took the bronze.

When Saleh put on a burst of speed at the very spot Rosa Mota had pulled away to win the women's race, Bordin began to see bronze again. Wakiihuri pulled ahead of him also and suddenly Bordin's goal became to stay ahead of Nakayama and bring a medal home for Italy.

Gelindo Bordin was born in 1959 in a town of a thousand people about fifty miles from Venice. He lived in a home shared with relatives and grew up as one of twenty-two children in the household. Bordin's family owned a vineyard, and he spent his summers washing out wine vats.

In 1973, Bordin entered a local road race. He had never trained and wore shoes that did not fit, but still finished fifth in a race of 700 runners. Over the next decade he gradually improved his running skills, constantly fighting battles against sickness and injury. Triumphs such as a third place finish in the national cross-country meet and a sixth place finish in the 10,000 meters at the World University Games were offset by back troubles, sickness, and finally that day in 1981 when he was left for dead by a motorist who hit him during a training run.

Doctors told him he would not be able to run for six months, but Bordin ignored their advice and was training again in three weeks. Enduring the pain of his injuries, Bordin recovered his conditioning within a few months. In 1984, he ran his first marathon in 2:13:20.

By 1985 Bordin had improved his personal best to 2:11:29 while placing twelfth at the World Cup. The next year he won the European Championships in spite of almost not qualifying for the Italian team.

Now, with a bronze medal in the World Championships, Bordin looked like a lock to take bronze again in the Olympics. He had been relaxed before the race, jogging for a few minutes and advising his old friend Ikangaa not to go out too fast.

Now, though, with the field down to three runners, Bordin was experiencing leg cramps and exhaustion. To provide a distraction from the threat of being overtaken by Nakayama, who was now running in fourth place, Bordin concentrated on Wakiihuri's back. "I was not thinking to catch him," he said later, "I just wanted to stay ahead of Nakayama."

With a mile and a half to go in the race, the course took a sharp turn. Looking at Wakiihuri across the corner of sidewalk, Bordin realized that he was actually gaining on the Kenyan. That realization was just the boost he needed to dig down and run a little faster. Just shy of twenty-five miles, he passed Wakiihuri. Now Bordin was running through his pain, while Saleh seemed to be suffering. Saleh glanced back frequently, clearly concerned that Bordin or Wakiihuri would overtake him. With just over a mile left in the race, Saleh looked back over his left shoulder and saw no challengers. When he looked over his right shoulder a few seconds later, Bordin smiled broadly. He was running just three yards behind. Fifty yards later, Bordin put on his own surge and breezed past Saleh.

"When I began to pass Saleh," he said, "I was thinking, 'Geez, the gold medal is just in front of me.' " Bordin crossed his heart, and ran harder than he believed he could run—finding within himself the extra surge that makes an Olympic champion.

With Saleh suffering now from not only physical pain, but the pain of having given up first place in the Olympic Marathon a mile from the finish, he made an easy target for Wakiihuri, who passed him a few hundred yards later. Bordin managed to hold off the charge from Wakiihuri and win the closest marathon in sixty-eight years, finishing just fifteen seconds ahead of the Kenyan. Saleh took third place twelve seconds later. In twentieth place, with a time of 2:16:15, was Dieudonne Lamothe of Haiti. The removal of the death threat that had hovered over his 1984 effort had helped turn him into a world-class runner.

Once again, the Olympic Marathon crowned an unexpected champion. Bordin later described the closing stages of the race as a war, telling reporters that he was too tired to be happy. But the Italian became an instant hero at home. He had, after all, erased the embarrassment of the strange finish by Dorando Pietri in 1908. Not since that time had an Italian even threatened to win the Olympic Marathon.

Bordin became immensely popular in Italy, not only because of his running success—after the Olympics he raced infrequently but almost always won—but also because of his lighthearted personality. A practical joker at heart, Bordin had dropped water balloons on security guards in the Olympic Village in Seoul, faked an accident during a training run with Bill Rodgers, and even fooled the Italian press into believing him when he announced his retirement on April 1, 1989.

As it had so often before, the Olympic Marathon in 1988 crowned a most unlikely of champions, but one who was truly worthy of the title. And Gelindo Bordin proved that the endurance and perseverance it takes to win the Olympic Marathon is not limited to the time of the race, but spans the life of an athlete.

23

The Games of the XXV Olympiad: Barcelona, 1992

If Seoul was notable for its lack of a major boycott, Barcelona will be remembered as the Games of the New World Order. One hundred and seventy-two nations, many of which had not existed four years earlier, competed in the Games. Germany fielded its first unified team since 1952. North Korea and Cuba returned to the Olympic fold after twelve years of absence. Many former Soviet republics fielded their own national teams, though the breakup of the Soviet Union had been so recent that some republics, without time to organize a team, banded together to send the "Unified Team," which would compete under the Olympic flag and hear the Olympic anthem played when its members won medals.

When the Games opened on July 25, a record 10,563 athletes marched into the stadium. Even South Africa had been invited back to the Olympic family after the abolishment of the apartheid system.

The Olympics had been conceived as an amateur competition, and had been conducted for many decades as such, but as the Games approached their centennial, the last vestiges of amateurism were slipping away. There was simply too much money involved in every aspect of the Olympics to expect that Olympic athletes could be amateurs. Most sports in the Barcelona Games opened the doors to professionals, with the most dramatic result being the total dominance of the American "Dream Team," in basketball. Where the Americans had previously fielded a group of college players, now the National Basketball Association all-stars, including Magic Johnson and Michael Jordan, would compete in the Olympics.

The marathon in Barcelona promised to be a gruelling affair. Not only would it be run in typical Summer Olympics heat and humidity, but the last stages of the course would be contested on the steep climb to Montjuic, where the Olympic Stadium was located. Never before had such a group of marathoners been assembled. Fifty-four of the starters had run marathons in under 2:12, twenty-two had bested 2:10. Defending champion Gelindo Bordin of Italy was in the race again, as were perennial favorites Ibrahim Hussein and Douglas Wakiihuri of Kenya. But this world-class group that assembled at the start knew the race would be one of endurance as much as speed. The survivor was likely to be the winner.

Many hoped to be that survivor, but many succumbed to heat, humidity, and other problems along the way. "It was a Who's Who of dead bodies,"[10] said American runner Ed Eyestone, who had chosen to run behind the leaders with his teammates, hoping enough runners would fade to give the Americans a chance at medalling. But for every great runner who could not maintain the pace, someone else stepped up. Hussein had stomach problems brought on by drinking too much water. World champion Hiromi Taniguchi of Japan got shoved at a water stop and then had his shoe stepped on.

"It fell off, but I did not surrender," Taniguchi said. "I kept chasing the pack and they kept moving away."

And so it went, with one runner after another succumbing to the heat, which had been 90°F at the start of the race, and the humidity, which was 72 percent at the finish.

The race began slowly, with the runners being cautious about starting too fast in hot weather and also with a head wind in their faces. In the early miles the lead pack numbered at least fifty. If anything, the pace slowed as the race went on. More runners caught up to the lead pack—the opposite of what one would expect. A pack of nearly sixty runners passed through the halfway point at 1:07:31. As the second half of the race got under way a parade of runners tried to pull into the lead—a parade that showed just how international this race was. Uniforms from Brazil, South Africa, Tanzania, Poland, Morocco, and Italy all took their turn at the front. All the while, though, the favorites remained cautiously in the middle of the pack, biding their time.

Koichi Morishita of Japan was the first runner to really push the pace when he surged ahead at the fifteen-mile mark and dropped the pace under five minutes per mile. Morishita had run only two marathons but he had won both of them and had a personal best of 2:08:53. He did not leave the pack alone, though. Another Asian runner, Hwang Young Cho of South Korea, could see gold as clearly as Morishita, and followed the lead of the Japanese runner.

As the two runners battled each other up the steep slopes of Montjuic, Hwang especially was aware of the symbolism of the moment. Fifty-six years earlier, Sohn Kee Chung, the great marathoner from Korea, had been forced to run under the flag of Japan. Sohn won the gold, but the record books show that medal going to a Japanese runner, not a Korean. Now, with a Korean battling a Japanese, eighty-year-old Sohn waited in the stands of the Olympic stadium to see which would emerge victorious.

Hwang had only been running marathons for a little over a year, though he had recorded a personal best of 2:08:47 in February to qualify for the Olympic race. Still, he was hardly a seasoned marathoner. His strategy had been to stay near the front until the last few miles, and then take off. So far that strategy had paid off, but he now found himself in a duel to decide the gold medal.

"When I was alone with the Japanese runner," Hwang said. "He kept looking at me, and I was nervous."

Hwang's nervousness didn't show. At the same time that he was worrying about Morishita, the Japanese runner was thinking how nice it would be to take home a silver medal.

Behind the two runners fighting their way up the hill, the massive lead pack had broken apart, and no one posed a threat to the leaders. The only runner to emerge from the remnants of the pack with any momentum was Germany's Stephan Freigang, who now ran solidly in third place.

Back on Montjuic, the history of the moment may have been too much for Morishita, or it might have been the weather or the hill. In any case, with a little over a mile left in the race, Hwang summoned his reserve and sprinted ahead. Morishita tried to respond, but he did not have the strength to go with Hwang.

Ironically, on this course that had been criticized for its vicious uphill at the end, Hwang pulled ahead on a slight downhill section. By the time the two reached the stadium, the margin had become 150 yards. Hwang won the gold medal for Korea in a time of 2:13:23. It had been the slowest Olympic Marathon since the altitude of Mexico City, but one of the most courageous in recent memory.

Hwang desperately wanted to run a victory lap, for Sohn as much as for himself, but it was not to be. In a scene reminiscent of Dorando Pietri's collapse in 1908, Hwang fell face down on the track after crossing the finish line. His leg was stiff with a painful cramp, and he vomited on the track—a victim of the intense weather conditions. He was carried off on a stretcher and soon recovered. His legs had felt fine while he was running, he later explained, but as soon as he stopped they had cramped badly.

Hwang was not the only runner needing medical attention. Four of the first five runners faltered after the finish, stumbling towards the shelter of the dressing rooms. Medical personnel were kept busy with a stream of exhausted runners. Dieudonne Lamothe, the Haitian runner whose Olympic career stretched back to 1976 and who finished the 1984 race under threat of death, had to be taken to a hospital following his participation in the gruelling marathon of Barcelona.

One hour and forty-five minutes after the winners finished, thirty-three-year-old Pyambuu Tuul of Mongolia approached a finish line that had been prepared for him on a warm-up track, because the stadium was being used for the Closing Ceremonies. Tuul was the only member of the Mongolian track and field team and the first person from his country ever to run the Olympic Marathon. Tuul had been blinded in a construction accident fourteen years earlier, but an operation paid for by the Achilles Track Club of New York had restored sight to his right eye in 1991. He completed the race in the darkness in a time of 4:00:44, nearly an hour after the penultimate finisher—but he finished. He was the final competitor of the Barcelona Games, but knew the same glory of participation as all the others.

Little was known about gold medalist Hwang, but he would want to leave the crowds of Barcelona knowing one thing about him—that he stood on the topmost step of the medal platform and received his gold while wearing the uniform of South Korea, and he stood proudly during the playing of his national anthem and thought of Sohn Kee Chung.

24

The Games of the XXVI Olympiad: Atlanta, 1996

From the moment that the president of the IOC, Juan Antonio Samaranch, announced that the Centennial Olympic Games had been awarded to Atlanta, Georgia, in a narrow decision over sentimental favorite Athens, Greece, American fans and athletes could feel the excitement. Atlanta became a city transformed by new athletic facilities, hotels, and a glorious park. These would truly be the Games of the people—with 11,000,000 tickets available, more than Barcelona and Seoul put together. Nearly 11,000 athletes would compete, more than ever before. And, for the first time in Olympic history, every country involved in the Olympic movement would send a team. Even a threatened boycott by North Korea was averted with some negotiations by Georgia native former President Jimmy Carter, and 197 national delegations paraded into Centennial Olympic Stadium on a glorious moonlit evening. The Atlanta Games were universal, and while the vicious bomb attack on Centennial Olympic Park that killed two people and injured over 100 on the day before the women's marathon changed the mood of the Games, it did anything but destroy the Olympics. In fact, it brought the spectators and athletes together even more than before, and made every participant in these Games—athletes, fans, coaches, officials, and volunteers—share in the experience of triumphing over adversity and fear.

That experience is one that Olympic marathoners know only too well, and while the fans of America rejoiced in the choice of Atlanta, world-class marathoners reacted in a different way to the IOC's announcement—they began immediately to dread the heat. The tradition in recent Olympics had been to have the men's marathon finish in the Olympic Stadium just before the Closing Ceremonies. In Atlanta this would mean a start time of 5:00 to 6:00 P.M. Temperatures at that time of day on August 4 could easily be in the nineties with high humidity. For this reason, the medical commission of the IOC recommended that the men compete in the early morning, as the women would. The IAAF, however, cited its own medical experts who claimed that late afternoon in Atlanta would be no worse than Barcelona. Juan Antonio Samaranch agreed, stating that he believed the race should be run in the late afternoon. As for the marathoners, some threatened to boycott the race, some began circulating petitions, and others referred to the race as a potential death march—a race that would be reduced to a survival contest. No one pointed out that the Olympic Marathon has traditionally been a survival contest run in unfavorable conditions.

On April 6, 1995, the IAAF announced that the men's race would start at 6:30 P.M., and while to many that seemed an improvement over the 5:00 P.M. start time that had been mentioned earlier, some racers still objected. Then, in December of 1995, the IAAF seemed ready to change its mind when its own chief medical officer announced that he recommended an early morning start. Finally, on March 24, 1996, the IAAF announced that the start time for the men's marathon would be 7:00 A.M. (In fact, it started at 7:05 A.M., to allow television coverage time to introduce the race.) The medals would still be awarded as a preamble to the Closing Ceremonies, but the race would start and finish in a near-empty stadium. Only die-hard marathon fans would pay to sit in the stands when they could watch the race for free on the streets of Atlanta.

One hundred years and nearly four months after the first Olympic marathon race, 122 runners lined up at Centennial Olympic Stadium to begin their own quest for gold. The marathon was the final event in a track and field competition that had seen world records fall in the men's 100 and 200 meters races, amazing double victories in the 200 and 400 meters races by Michael Johnson of the United States and Marie Jose Pérec of France, and the first Olympic medal awarded to a black South African when Hezekiel Sepeng took the silver in the greatest 800 meters race ever run.

In 1896, runners had pounded out the marathon on dirt roads with horses and bicycles as companions. They had stopped for water and even wine as refreshment when the opportunity presented itself. News of the race had been relayed to the stadium by those same bicyclists and horse riders. In 1996, the runners would be preceded by a convoy of more than a dozen natural gas and electric-powered trucks. Replacement drinks they had prepared for their personal taste ahead of time would wait for them on designated tables along the route. Their progress would be monitored in the stadium on a giant television screen and broadcast throughout the world from cameras on motorcycles, golf carts, and a dozen helicopters that hovered above the leaders throughout the race. Still, the runners faced the same challenge that their precursors faced—survival and victory.

In the 100 years since the inception of the marathon, the race had evolved and grown to monstrous proportions. Now, unlike the Olympic race, most marathons include thousands of competitors. The absence of one runner in particular makes the complexion of the Olympic Marathon different from that of others. Most organizers of major marathon races hire a rabbit—a runner who is paid to run a fast pace over the first half of the race, pulling the field along and increasing the possibility that records will be set. In the Atlanta Olympic Marathon, there was no rabbit—only 122 world-class runners, a phenomenally talented field that would have to use strategy and tactics as much as speed and endurance to win this race.

Absent from the race was the defending champion Hwang Young Cho, who was suffering from an ankle injury and had finished only twenty-ninth in an Olympic trial race. The pre-race favorites included Martin Fiz, the world champion from Spain who had had the fastest time of the year up to the Olympics; German Silva of Mexico, twice winner of the New York City Marathon; and Lee Bong-Ju of Korea, who had lost a marathon to Fiz by one second earlier in the year. All the favorites had one thing in common— they had demonstrated an ability to run well in hot conditions.

The Atlanta race began in the fog. Heat was not a major factor, but the 90 percent humidity certainly was. The runners made three circuits of the track, then headed out onto the hilly streets of Atlanta to follow a painted blue line on the streets for twenty-five miles. The course wound through downtown Atlanta, past the birthplace of Martin Luther King, Jr., and out Peachtree Road to Oglethorpe University, where it turned around, following Peachtree back to downtown before turning toward the stadium and the finish.

The lack of a rabbit was noticed almost immediately, as no one seemed willing to force the early pace and a massive lead pack of over fifty runners pushed along through the streets. Two runners from Poland took a lead of a stride or two as the race passed by the skyscrapers of Atlanta, but no serious breaks were made. The tension among runners and fans alike was clear— who would make a break and when?

The pack remained essentially intact through the turnaround point. On a long gradual downhill after Oglethorpe, the pace began to quicken and at about the sixteen-mile point, Lee Bong-Ju of Korea surged ahead of the pack. His break was quickly covered by all three runners from South Africa, and despite opening up a five-second advantage over the field, they were soon caught by the chase pack led by Martin Fiz. Lee's move had pushed the pace, though, and the lead pack was now down to twenty runners.

Not until the nineteen-mile point did the move come that finally forced the disintegration of the lead pack. Josia Thugwane of South Africa made a slight surge, pulling into the lead by several yards. His move was covered by Lee Bong-Ju, and soon the two runners had opened up a gap of seven seconds on the field.

Josia Thugwane was lucky to be in Atlanta at all. He was from a country that, until recently, had not permitted black and white athletes on the same playing field, a country that had been excluded from the Olympics from 1964 through 1988. And, unlike Kenneth McArthur, the South African who had won the marathon in 1912, Thugwane was black. But the real sign of how lucky Thugwane was to be in this race was an inch-long scar along his chin. In March he had stopped his car to pick up a friend and four strangers jumped in. They took his keys and pulled a gun on him. Thugwane jumped from the car as it sped away, a bullet grazing his chin. In spite of a back injury, he was able to train with the South African team in Albequerque, New Mexico in June.

Thugwane, a security guard at a coal mine and the father of four girls, had started his athletic career as a soccer player. He tried distance running for the first time in 1988. He won the equivalent of about $18 in his first road race and decided to turn all his efforts to running. He had won the Cape Town Marathon earlier in 1996 and the Honolulu Marathon, another hot weather affair, the year before. Now Thugwane, whose five-foot-two-inch, ninety-nine-pound body looked more like a gymnast's than a marathoner's, was trying to pull away from Lee Bong-Ju in the final stages of the Centennial Olympic Marathon.

At the twenty-mile mark, Thugwane and Lee had a nine-second lead on the remnants of the pack, which still included Martin Fiz, and their lead seemed to be growing. The battle now appeared to be for the bronze. Then, just past the twenty-mile mark, Eric Wainaina, a twenty-two year old Kenyan, pulled away from Fiz and put on a surge of his own, catching Thugwane and Lee within a few hundred yards. By twenty-one miles, the medal winners seemed to be set, but the order was far from certain. Over the next few miles, each of the runners put on a surge, trying the break away from the other two, and each time the others closed the gap again. The spectators in the stadium began to think they might see the race decided on the track for the first time since 1948. Past the twenty-five-mile mark, it was

Thugwane who put on a spurt, opening up a ten-yard lead, but Lee caught him and moved into the lead.

With the stadium in sight and a little over a half-mile left in the race, the course made a right turn into a short downhill stretch. Here Thugwane surged once more, sprinting down the hill and finally breaking away from Lee. Wainaina, too, took advantage of the downhill to pass Lee as the three raced toward the stadium. Thugwane entered first, but only about twenty yards behind him, Lee passed Wainaina in the tunnel to move into second place. The runners now had one circuit of the track plus the length of a straightaway left in the race. All three ran hard and strong around the track, but though Lee closed the gap slightly, the places remained as they were. With twenty yards to go Thugwane waved his arms above his head in celebration. He crossed the finish line in 2:12:26 to become the first black South African to win an Olympic gold medal. Three seconds later, Lee took the silver and five seconds after that Wainaina finished. It had been the closest marathon finish in Olympic history. In the women's race of 1992, eight seconds had separated gold from silver. In this race, the same gap separated gold from bronze. The closest previous finish in the men's race had been Hannes Kohlemainen's thirteen-second victory over Jüri Loss-mann in 1920.

Martin Fiz finished in fourth place, forty-four seconds behind Thugwane. Richard Nerurkar of Great Britain took fifth and German Silva of Mexico sixth. In spite of all the worries about weather, the heat played much less of a role than it had in Barcelona four years earlier. Of 122 starters, 111 finished, and while the heat and humidity clearly took its toll on some runners, it was ultimately strategy and strength, not weather, that deter-mined the outcome of this race. Even though the course had more vertical climbing than the 1992 Barcelona course, the times of the top four runners were all faster than the winner's time in Barcelona.

In an Olympics that began with a tribute to Dr. Martin Luther King, Jr. at the Opening Ceremonies, it seemed tremendously appropriate that the final medal ceremony saw the raising of the South African flag to honor a black athlete. In a tribute to Nelson Mandela and to the victory of his homeland over apartheid, Thugwane announced after the race that he had won the gold medal for his country and his president.

There is one more story to be told about the 1996 marathon—a story that illustrates the spirit of the Olympic Games as well as any tale of victory. The last of the 111 finishers to cross the finish line was Abdul-Baser Wasiqui, one of three athletes in the delegation to the 1996 Games from Afghanistan. Wasiqui had run a 2:28 marathon in Hamburg to set the Afghan national record and qualify for the Olympics. He was the first athlete from his country to compete in an Olympic marathon. During the race in Atlanta, he had suffered from severe cramping and had slowed to a walk for much of the second half of the course. But, in the spirit of Coubertin's belief that participation is more important than victory, Wasiqui refused to drop out of the race. He continued on toward the stadium for more than two hours after the winners crossed the finish line. When he had been running about four hours, Olympic officials announced that he would have to finish on the warm-up track, as Pyambuu Tuul had done in Barcelona in 1992. The stadium was being prepared for the Closing Ceremonies and the blue tarp that covered the track for that occasion had already been pulled into place. A few minutes later, perhaps inspired by Coubertin, the officials reversed themselves. Volunteers who were preparing for that night's ceremonies pulled the tarp back off the track and cheered when Wasiqui walked into the stadium. The spectators were long gone, but the hundreds of volunteers whose spirits had been so high throughout these games lined the track applauding one last athlete. As Wasiqui headed for the finish line, volunteers stretched out a tape for him to break and crowded around to shake his hand. He finished the race in 4:24:17, the slowest recorded time in Olympic Marathon history, a distinction that had previously been held by 1908 finisher George Lister of Canada.

For his efforts as a participant in the 1996 Olympic Games, Wasiqui received what every Olympic competitor has received since 1896, a participant's medal. Though less publicized than the gold, silver, and bronze medals that go to Olympic victors, the participant's medal carries with it no less glory for an athlete like Wasiqui. His courage and perseverance embodied all that the Olympics can be at their best, and all those who watched his effort—on the roads of Atlanta, in the Olympic Stadium, or on television—thought him no less a champion than the man who finished first.

Part II

The Women's Race

25

The Fight to Establish the Women's Race

By the 1970s, the Olympic Marathon had come a long way from the dusty roads of Athens. Yet women were still not allowed to compete and the struggle to establish a women's Olympic Marathon was itself something of a long-distance race.

Before the 1980s, there were no women's distance races in the Olympics. In the Moscow Games, the longest race for women was the 1,500 meters, which had been instituted in 1972. Women had been excluded from track and field competition altogether until 1928, when the longest race was the 800 meters. Despite a world record by winner Lina Radke of Germany, many of the competitors had not properly prepared for the race and several collapsed in exhaustion. This led Olympic organizers to consider the race too strenuous for women. The president of the IOC, Count Henri Baillet-Latour, even suggested the elimination of all women's competition from the Games. Such a drastic move was not taken, but until 1960, when the 800 meters reappeared, no race of over 200 meters was contested by women in the Olympics.

This is not to say there was no tradition of women's long-distance running. Women had been forbidden from participating in the ancient Olympics. A woman who was caught even as a spectator at the Games could face execution. But women in ancient Greece held their own festival to honor the goddess Hera every five years. Only one athletic event was held—a short footrace.

When the Olympics were revived in 1896, women were again excluded. But, in March of 1896, Stamatis Rovithi became the first woman to run a marathon when she covered the proposed Olympic course from Marathon to Athens. The following month, a woman named Melpomene presented herself as an entrant in the Olympic Marathon. Race organizers denied her the opportunity to compete. Undiscouraged, Melpomene warmed up for the race out of sight. When the starter's gun sounded, she began to run along the side of the course. Eventually she fell behind the men, but as she continued on, stopping at Pikermi for a glass of water, she passed runners who had dropped out of the race in exhaustion. She arrived at the stadium about an hour and a half after Spiridon Louis won the race. Barred from entry into the now empty stadium, she ran her final lap around the outside of the building, finishing in approximately four and a half hours. One Greek newspaper wrote that the Olympic organizers were discourteous to disallow Melpomene's entry into the race, but nonetheless it would be nearly a century before another woman would run the Olympic Marathon.

Violet Piercy of Great Britain was the first woman to be officially timed in the marathon, when she clocked a time of 3:40:22 in a British race on October 3, 1926. Due largely to the lack of women's marathon competition, that time stood as an unofficial world record for thirty-seven years. On December 16, 1963, American Merry Lepper ran a time of 3:37:07 to improve slightly on Piercy's record. Still, no highly competitive times were recorded simply because there was no women's competition in the race.

Before 1972, women had been barred from the most famous marathon outside the Olympics—Boston. That rule did not keep women from running, though. In 1966, Roberta Gibb hid behind a bush at the start of the Boston Marathon, sneaking into the field and finishing the race in an unofficial time of 3:21:25. She was the first woman known to complete the arduous Boston course. Gibb had been inspired to run by the return of her race entry with a note saying that women were not physically capable of running a marathon.

"I hadn't intended to make a feminist statement," said Gibb. "I was running against the distance [not the men] and I was measuring myself with my own potential."[11]

The following year, number 261 in the Boston Marathon was assigned to entrant K. V. Switzer. In lieu of the pre-race medical examination, Switzer's coach took a health certificate to race officials and picked up the number. Not until two miles into the race did officials realize that Switzer was a woman, twenty-year-old Kathrine Switzer of Syracuse University. Race director Will Cloney and official Jock Semple tried to grab Switzer and remove her from the race, or at least remove her number, but her teammates from Syracuse fended them off with body blocks. Switzer eventually finished the race after the race timers had stopped running, in 4:20. Switzer had not used her initials on the entry form to deceive the race officials. She was merely a fan of J. D. Salinger and liked the sound of her initials. While Switzer was creating a stir with her unauthorized entry, Roberta Gibb again ran the race, this time being forced off the course just steps from the finish line, where her time would have been 3:27:17.

The photographs of race officials chasing after Switzer that appeared in the national papers the next day brought the issue of women's long-distance running to the public. Race officials defended their actions, saying they were only enforcing rules that forbade men and women from competing in the same race and barred women from races of more than one and a half miles.

"I think it's time to change the rules," said Switzer. "They are archaic."[12] Switzer's story and the surrounding publicity had made the quest for equality in road racing for women a political issue. Coming as it did in the midst of the women's liberation movement, it galvanized women in the belief that it was time, as Switzer had said, to change the rules.

Slowly, the rules did begin to change. On August 31, 1971, Adrienne Beames of Australia became the first woman to run a sub-three-hour marathon, smashing that barrier with a time of 2:46:30. In 1972, women were allowed to compete officially in the Boston Marathon for the first time. As running became a more popular sport during the 1970s, more women began competing in marathons.

On October 28, 1973, the first all women's marathon was held in Waldniel, West Germany. The success of that race was built on the following October when Dr. Ernst Van Aaken, a West German and a strong supporter of women's running, sponsored the first Women's International Marathon Championship in Waldniel. Forty women from seven countries competed in the event. Two years later, when the race was held again, the forty-five finishers represented nine different countries. Still, with the 1980 Summer Olympic Games on the horizon, Olympic organizers had given no serious consideration to creating a women's marathon.

Two reasons were often given for this exclusion. First, some experts claimed that women's health would be damaged by long-distance running. This theory was proved false not only by medical studies, but also by the success of women marathoners during the 1970s. Second, the Olympic Charter stated that to be included in the Games, a women's sport must be widely practiced in at least twenty-five countries on at least two continents (for men's events the requirement was fifty countries on three continents).

Women's marathoning, the Olympic organizers argued, was simply not popular enough to include.

In the late 1970s, Kathrine Switzer, retired from competitive running, led the way toward the inclusion of a women's marathon in the Olympics. In 1977, Switzer, then director of the Women's Sports Foundation, met an executive for the Avon cosmetics company who told her the company was interested in sponsoring a running event for women. Switzer wrote a seventy-five page proposal describing how Avon might sponsor a series of events, and the company liked her idea so much they hired her to plan the races.

The first Avon International Marathon was held in Atlanta, Georgia, in March of 1978, drawing women from nine countries. The 1979 Avon Marathon, held in Waldniel, attracted over 250 world class entrants from twenty-five countries. The theory that women's marathoning was not popular enough to become an Olympic sport was dramatically disproved. Still, the drive for inclusion in the Olympics was far from over.

Norwegian runner Grete Waitz won the women's division of the New York City Marathon in 1979 for the second year in a row, crossing the finish line in a time of 2:27:33. She thus became the first woman to run the distance in under 2:30. The *New York Times* ran an editorial pointing out that in just fifteen years the women's record had been lowered by one hour. In that same editorial, the *Times* called for the creation of an Olympic Marathon for women. Although Waitz herself was not active in the drive to create a women's Olympic Marathon, her successes were often cited by supporters of the race.

In 1979, marathoner Jaqueline Hansen, who had broken the 2:40 barrier in 1975, teamed with other runners from around the world to form the International Runners Committee to lobby for the inclusion of women's long-distance races in international competition. The committee received support from the Nike shoe company, which ran full-page advertisements in several running magazines calling for a women's Olympic Marathon. The marathon was not the only race being supported, however. The race that seemed to have the best chance for inclusion in the 1984 Games was the 3,000 meters. Some lobbyists felt that the addition of women's races should be made gradually, with the 3,000 meters being added first, followed by the 5,000 meters, 10,000 meters, and then the marathon.

A central player in the drive for the inclusion of women's distance races in the Olympics was Adriaan Paulen, president of IAAF. One of the responsibilities of the IAAF is recommending new track and field events to the IOC. When the IAAF Congress met in San Juan, Puerto Rico in 1979, Paulen pointed out that he had long been fighting to get the women's 3,000 meters included in the Olympics. But, he warned that fighting for other races at the same time might weaken the case for the 3,000 meters or any distance race to be added. "Take things one step at a time" seemed to be the conventional wisdom.

Meanwhile, on the roads the case for a women's Olympic Marathon was slowly building. Not only had the Avon races brought international attention and participation to the sport, but the women's marathon was becoming legitimate in other ways as well. The race had received sanction by the American Amateur Athletic Union (AAU) in 1972, and the AAU's first national marathon for women had been held in 1974. More importantly, the IAAF, an international rather than national organization, had made plans to include women's marathon competitions at future World Cup meets, beginning at the 1981 meet in Rome, and at the World Track and Field Championships beginning in 1983. The 1982 European Marathon Championships, another IAAF event, which would be run on the historic Marathon to Athens course, would also include a women's division. Though the IAAF was not ready to recommend the marathon to the IOC, it was poised to sanction the race in its own meets. Paulen hoped that the inclusion of the women's marathon in these prestigious international meets would lure runners from Eastern European countries into women's marathoning. Opposition from the Soviet Bloc had been one obstacle to Olympic sanction.

The first women's marathon officially sanctioned by the IAAF was the Tokyo International, held in November of 1979. IAAF president Adriaan Paulen travelled to Tokyo to watch the race. To the surprise of many who had lobbied Paulen before, he was so impressed by the level of competition in Tokyo that he announced he would fully support the effort to institute a women's marathon in the Olympics and that he would lobby for 5,000 meters and 10,000 meters races as well. A short time later, the IAAF officially recommended to the IOC that a women's marathon be included in the 1984 Los Angeles Olympics.

Although endorsement by the IAAF was an important step toward the establishment of a women's marathon, many obstacles had yet to be overcome. One official from the Los Angeles planning committee claimed the Games were already too big for the inclusion of more events. An official with the IOC argued that the effects of marathon running on women's health needed further study.

This second argument was rebutted by the American College of Sports Medicine (ACSM) in January of 1980 when it issued an opinion statement saying that "there exists no conclusive scientific or medical evidence that long-distance running is contraindicated for the healthy, trained female athlete. The ACSM recommends that females be allowed to compete at the national and international level in the same distances in which their male counterparts compete."[13]

Powerful people were in favor of the new marathon, too. On the floor of the United States Senate, Sen. Nancy Kassebaum of Kansas introduced a resolution calling for the Senate's support of an Olympic Marathon and other long-distance races for women. Both Adriaan Paulen and president of the IOC Lord Killanin made personal statements in support of the race to the members of the IOC when the committee met during the Moscow Games in July of 1980. The question of creating the new marathon race was deferred until the meeting of the IOC's Executive Board, however, in February of 1981.

In the meantime, the third Avon International Marathon was held in London on the final day of the Moscow Olympics. Women from twenty-seven countries competed, and for the first time in history, five women finished below the 2:40 barrier.

"Obviously, we think it's time a women's marathon was made part of the Olympics," said Kathrine Switzer, again the organizer of the race. "We're trying to prove to people that women are just as suited, or even more suitable, for marathoning as men."[14]

Switzer traveled to Los Angeles in February of 1981 when the Executive Board of the IOC was scheduled to meet. She knew the vote on the race could be close. The Board was made up of nine countries, eight of which were represented at the meeting. The Soviet Union openly opposed the creation of the race, and Switzer feared that Panama and Romania would side with their political ally. Spain, Japan, India, and New Zealand favored the race. Belgium appeared undecided. Five votes were needed for the resolution to pass.

On the morning of February 23, Switzer went to the hotel where the meeting was being held. Unsure what she could do to further her cause, she approached the delegate from Belgium in the hall and began to tell him all about the success of women's marathoning—the number of women competing, the quality of their races, their good health. The delegate took careful notes and then disappeared into the meeting.

Unable to stand still while she waited for the result, Switzer went out for a six-mile run. At 6:30 that evening, the Executive Board of IOC announced that a women's marathon had been given its approval and would likely be included in the 1984 Summer Games in Los Angeles. The committee had even decided to ignore a rule stating that all new events had to be approved four years in advance of their inclusion in the Games. The Soviet Union was the only country to vote against the race. The struggle was almost over. All that remained was approval of the Executive Board's recommendation by the full membership of the IOC.

In September of 1981, the IOC met in Baden-Baden, Germany and made several important decisions. They elected the first women members of that body in its eighty-four year history. After a powerful speech by middle-distance runner Sebastian Coe they voted to allow the ruling federations for each Olympic sport set their own requirements for Olympic eligibility, clearing the way for marathoners and other athletes to receive prize and endorsement money while still remaining eligible for Olympic competition. In the midst of all these decisions, they voted on the recommendation of the Executive Board concerning the women's marathon race. Lost in the headlines about the end of amateurism at the Olympics and the selection of Seoul and Calgary for the 1988 Games was the fact that women had finally won the right to compete in an Olympic Marathon.

26

The Games of the XXIII Olympiad: Los Angeles, 1984

Following as it did the long battle for inclusion in Olympic competition, the race that took place on August 5, 1984 was something like a victory lap for all women marathoners. Among the favored starters were Norwegian Grete Waitz, who had never lost a marathon she had finished; Portugal's Rosa Mota, who had won the marathon in the European Championships in 1982; and American Joan Benoit, who had set the world record of 2:22:43 in the Boston Marathon in 1983. Waitz, who had lowered the woman's record many times and had run the first sub-2:30 marathon, had never met Benoit in a marathon race.

Benoit was born in Cape Elizabeth, Maine, in 1957. Her earliest athletic passion was skiing, taught to her by her father who had been an army skier during World War II. As a high school sophomore she broke her leg on the slopes. As part of her recovery from that accident she began to run and she found that she liked running just as much as skiing.

In college she played field hockey while continuing to run. When she showed up at practice one day sore from a thirteen-mile run the day before, the coach made her sit out the rest of the season and Benoit quit the team and started running full time. In 1979 she entered the Boston Marathon, her second marathon ever, as a Bowdoin College senior and won the women's division, setting an American record in the process.

After graduation, Benoit worked as the women's track and cross-country coach at Boston University while she continued to train 100 miles a week.

With the promise of the first ever women's Olympic Marathon in 1984, Benoit hoped to be in her best shape ever so she could make a run for the gold.

As she lined up for the start of the Olympic race, though, Benoit felt lucky to be in the field at all. Seventeen days before the Olympic trials she had undergone knee surgery. She recovered quickly and won the qualifying race to secure one of three spots on the American team. Benoit and the two other qualifiers, Julie Brown and Julie Isphording, each received a bronze figurine of a running woman for their success in the Olympic trials. Fittingly, the sculpture was created by none other than Roberta Gibb, who had broken the gender barrier of the Boston Marathon so many years before.

On June 17, Benoit had won the Olympic Trials Exhibition 10,000 meters race by an impressive margin. Unlike the marathon, the 10,000 meters had not yet been approved for women's competition in the Olympics, though it would be on the program four years later in Seoul.

Benoit traveled to Los Angeles several days before the Games began, but her recent appearance on television made it impossible for her to take training runs without being recognized. After the Opening Ceremonies, the private Benoit flew to Eugene, Oregon, to stay with friends and prepare for the race. Four days later she was back in Los Angeles. She had a near-sleepless night on August 4, and then the day that women runners had been campaigning for for so long finally dawned.

The athletes marched onto the track by nation in alphabetical order, with the United States entering last as the host country. With the athletes in each delegation arranged by height, tiny Joan Benoit was the final runner to enter the Santa Monica College stadium, starting point of the marathon.

Fifty competitors from twenty-eight nations left Santa Monica College at 8:00 A.M. and began to make their way through twenty-six miles of warm muggy Los Angeles. Ironically, the field was deeper than it might have been if the political struggles of women's long-distance runners had been more successful. The marathon and the 3,000 meters were still the only long-distance races for women in the Olympics. A lawsuit brought by the American Civil Liberties Union and the International Runners Committee to force the inclusion of 5,000 and 10,000 meter races in the 1984 Games had been unsuccessful. So, on the morning of August 5, the greatest women's distance runners in the world took to the streets of Los Angeles. Some were 5,000 meter specialists, some preferred the 10,000 meters, and many were best at the marathon, but all made history.

Olympic marathons are usually races of many lead changes and careful tactics. Well thought out pacing and strategically calculated surges help competitors toward victory. In the first women's Olympic Marathon, how-ever, only one tactical decision affected the race for the gold medal. A mere fourteen minutes into the race, American Joan Benoit, who felt the pace was too slow, pulled ahead of the rest of the pack.

"I did not want to take the lead," said Benoit afterward, "but I promised myself I'd run my race and nobody else's and that's exactly what I did. I didn't have any second thoughts."[15] Shortly after she pulled away, the runners came to the first water stop, but Benoit had no interest in getting tangled back up in the pack, so she skipped it.

To many, Benoit's move may have looked foolish. After all, a marathoner needs other competitors to push her along. How could Benoit possibly keep up a winning pace running all alone? But her lead widened over the next several miles, and none of the other runners made an attempt to go after her. They all assumed she was over-extending herself and that the heat would eventually break her, but Benoit was running comfortably and increasing her lead with every stride. The picture of the lone woman in her white painter's cap would become the indelible image of this historic race. At five miles, she had a thirteen-second lead over the other runners. By the nineteen-mile mark, that lead had grown to two minutes, and she had built that lead during the coolest part of the race. Now the runners in the second place pack, Waitz, her teammate Ingrid Kristiansen, and Rosa Mota, had to catch Benoit in the increasing heat of the day.

Though Grete Waitz would close the gap slightly, her effort would come too late. The race would finish on the track in the Los Angeles Coliseum, which was serving as Olympic stadium for the second time. With that building in sight, Benoit passed by a giant mural of her victory in the 1983 Boston Marathon. The painting, on the side of a building, had been com-missioned by Nike. Though slightly embarrassed by the painting, Benoit felt inspired too. Now, she was close to winning another, much more important marathon. Passing through the tunnel that led into the Olympic Stadium, Benoit realized that her life was about to change completely.

"Once you leave this tunnel," she told herself, "your life will be changed forever." Of course, it was too late to turn back. Benoit emerged into the roar of the coliseum and told herself to look straight ahead. "You're not finished," she thought, "Get around the track and nail this thing down."[16] And she kept on going, unfazed by the 77,000 cheering fans who welcomed her entrance onto the Olympic track. With 200 yards to go, she finally cracked her grim reserve and waved her hat at the crowd, smiling broadly. She finished in 2:24:52, the third fastest women's marathon ever and a time that would have won thirteen of the twenty previous men's Olympic marathons. Grete Waitz finished second in 2:26:18, and Rosa Mota sur-prised everyone by finishing third, crossing the finish line thirty-nine seconds later. Mota had surged past Kristiansen at the twenty-mile mark and was able to maintain a lead over the Norwegian to win the bronze in a personal best time of 2:26:57.

Waitz remarked later that while her own performance had been good, Benoit's had been great.

Benoit later admitted that the race had been very easy for her. After appearances on all three major television networks, Benoit flew home to Maine three days after the marathon, anxious to return to her quiet life and avoid the spotlight that had fallen on her at the Olympics. But Joan Benoit (now Joan Samuelson) did find that her life was changed by winning the first women's Olympic Marathon. She became the idol of millions of American women who run. Just as Frank Shorter had touched off a running boom by his victory in 1972, which showed American men the excitement and reward of long-distance running, Joan Benoit legitimized the efforts of all those women who strove to follow in her footsteps. She became, in a single morning, the leader of the American women's running movement and a worldwide celebrity. It can be said with some confidence that Joan Benoit was to women's running in America in the 1980s what Spiridon Louis was to Greek pride in the 1890s. But to herself, she would always be a simple, private person who loved to run. Back in her native Maine, she married her college sweetheart. In 1985 in Chicago, she set another American record in the marathon, running 2:21:21.

The most dramatic finish of the race was not Benoit's impressive victory, but the finish of Swiss competitor Gabriele Andersen-Scheiss, who entered the stadium fifteen minutes later suffering from heat exhaustion. The crowd gasped in horror as Andersen-Scheiss staggered onto the track, her torso twisted, her right arm straight and her left arm limp, her right knee strangely stiff. She waved away medical personnel who rushed to help her knowing that, if they touched her, she, like Dorando Pietri seventy-six years earlier, would be disqualified. For nearly six minutes Andersen-Scheiss hobbled around the track, occasionally stopping and holding her head. Doctors watched her carefully and determined she was in no immediate danger. She collapsed over the finish line in thirty-seventh place into the arms of waiting medics. Fortunately, Andersen-Scheiss recovered quickly. Her time of 2:48:45 would have won the gold medal in the first five Olympic marathons.

An embarrassing note to the women's race of 1984 concerned Leda Diaz de Cano of Honduras. In the midst of world-class competition, de Cano fell behind immediately, trailing by over six minutes just three miles into the race. By the nine-mile mark she was last by nearly a half-hour, and officials convinced her to drop out. Coubertin's credo of the importance of taking part had given way to the importance of keeping to the schedule on the track and allowing cars back on the freeways of Los Angeles.

Kathrine Switzer had not disappeared from the running scene when the women ran their historic race in Los Angeles. She was beginning a new career as a sports commentator and watched Joan Benoit's dramatic finish on a television monitor while working for ABC television.

Women marathoners had arrived at the Olympics and no one doubted their right to be there. From the remarkable solo performance of American gold-medal winner Joan Benoit to the dramatic courage of Gabriele Andersen-Scheiss, the first women's Olympic Marathon was an event no Olympic spectator would soon forget.

27

The Games of the XXIV Olympiad: Seoul, 1988

The women's race in Seoul was perhaps as notable for its absentees as for its participants. Defending gold medalist Joan Benoit Samuelson had recovered from giving birth and from a back injury, but still chose not to run in the Olympic trials. Ingrid Kristiansen, who had placed fourth in the 1984 marathon, had achieved the remarkable feat of setting the world record in the 5,000 meters, 10,000 meters, and marathon since the last Olympics. In the Seoul Games, however, she chose to concentrate her efforts on the 10,000 meters, so she did not enter the marathon.

What the Seoul race did have was an overwhelming favorite—Rosa Mota of Portugal, who had won the bronze medal in 1984. Mota had been a tremendously consistent marathoner in the two years leading up to the Olympics, not only winning races, but generally winning them by margins of several minutes. Her personal best of 2:23:29 was the best of anyone in the 1988 Olympic field. Of the twelve marathons she had run, she had won nine.

Mota began her marathoning career in 1982. Despite warnings from Portuguese officials to her coach not to enter "a little girl" in the marathon, Mota ran the marathon at the European Championships and won. Unfazed by her first marathon, Mota went for a run with friends after the race. In Los Angeles in 1984 she became the first Portuguese woman to win an Olympic medal when she took the bronze in the inaugural women's Olympic Marathon. She had not heard the last from Portuguese running officials, however. They were less than pleased with Mota's independent mindedness, and threatened to keep her out of the Olympics. In the end, though, nothing would stop her from competing in Seoul. Even the heat, which threatened to be a factor as always, never seemed to affect Mota.

Mota was a popular runner with her competitors because of her carefree attitude about racing. Her coach and companion Jose Pedrosa said that he and Rosa ran for fun.

A relaxed, good natured marathoner, Mota was a modest competitor despite all her success. Still, even she felt confident in her ability to strike gold in Seoul. "I am more experienced, stronger and know the other runners better than I did in '84. I don't consider myself the favorite, but I am one of the ones who can win."[17] The other runners included Grete Waitz of Norway, who had so dominated the early years of women's marathoning and who had placed second in Los Angeles; Lisa Martin of Australia, the seventh place finisher in 1984 and the woman whom Joan Benoit Samuelson picked as the winner; Lorraine Moller of New Zealand, along with Waitz the most experienced marathoner in the field; Zoya Ivanova, who won the World Cup race on the Seoul course in 1987; and Katrin Dörre of East Germany, who, despite rumors to the contrary, was *not* pregnant.

Rosa Mota might be an easy-going runner, but she was not one to enter a race without a plan. In Seoul she planned to win the gold, and her coach Jose Pedrosa helped her figure out how. A week before the race he picked the point where she should surge ahead of anyone still running with her. That spot was a small hill, something of an anomaly on this flat course. He showed Mota this spot just before the twenty-four mile mark and they agreed that that would be where the gold medal would be won.

Seventy-two starters lined up at 9:30 A.M. on September 23. Ria van Landeghem of Belgium was not one of them. Van Landeghem had been sent home by Belgium officials after failing a controversial pre-race drug test. Although she had passed four drug tests in the months leading up to the Games, and passed two more shortly after returning to her home in Boulder, Colorado, team officials informed her that her urine sample in Seoul contained the drug nandrolone. When she asked that the sample be tested again, they came back with another answer—this time, they said, it contained oxandrolone, a different forbidden drug. Despite the inconsistencies in the drug test, van Landeghem, who had feuded in the past with Belgian officials over her decision to live and train in the United States, was kicked off the team, and her dream of being an Olympian was shattered.

But the race went on, and from the beginning it was evident that Rosa Mota was determined to win. Mota, Martin, Dörre, and Soviet runner Tatyana Polovinskaya took turns leading the early stages of the race. Mota tried to break away several times, hoping she might put the race away early as Joan Benoit had four years earlier, but the other three stuck with her through the surges. As the race wore on, Mota waited for the assigned spot to make her move. By then she was running with Martin and Dörre only. The Soviet runner had dropped back a mile earlier.

At the top of the hill they had staked out earlier, Mota saw her coach, who had been getting around that morning on his bicycle in order to offer her encouragement. He reminded her that this was the time, but Mota needed no reminding, and when she surged ahead at the designated slope, the other two runners couldn't stay with her.

"I just couldn't," said Martin. "I was prepared to do whatever Rosa did, and when she pulled away I knew I should go with her. But I was already so tired that I couldn't."[18]

By the time she had gone up and over the hill, Mota had opened up a 50-yard lead. When she reached the stadium, the lead was 150 yards. Mota won in a time of 2:25:40, and was greeted at the finish by her coach, who had vaulted out of the stands and over the photographers to meet her on the track. Lisa Martin held on for the silver medal and Katrin Dörre took the bronze. Grete Waitz had dropped out of the race at the eighteen-mile mark, apparently suffering the after effects of knee surgery she had had forty-six days earlier.

Were there any surprises in the 1988 women's Olympic Marathon? Well, for the first time in Olympic history a heavy favorite had won a marathon using exactly the strategy devised before the race and the other medals had been taken by favored runners. In the long history of marathon finishes, those facts alone must come as something of a surprise.

28

The Games of the XXV Olympiad: Barcelona, 1992

Shortly before the start of the 1992 women's Olympic Marathon, the medical director of the race took the road temperature on the course—113°F. That fact alone explains why this was the slowest women's Olympic race yet run. It would take a time of only 2:32:41 to win the gold.

Over fifty years earlier, on the night of January 24, 1939, the women of Barcelona had fled the encroaching forces of General Franco and escaped on the coastal road out of the city. Now, another group of women would travel that road, this time in peace, travelling into the city instead of away from it.

Unlike in 1988, there was no clear-cut favorite in the 1992 race. Rosa Mota had dropped out of the field a week before the Games complaining of stomach pains. Leading the pack of contenders was Lisa Martin Ondieki of Australia. As Lisa Martin, she had placed seventh in the Los Angeles Olympics and then taken the silver medal in Seoul. Since that time, she had married Yobes Ondieki, a Kenyan who served as her coach. The month before the Olympics, Ondieki had lowered her personal best in the 10,000 meters by a full minute. In the marathon, her personal best was three minutes faster than anyone else in the Barcelona field.

Also returning from the 1988 Games was Katrin Dörre, now of Germany rather than East Germany. The U.S. hopes were led by Francie Larrieu-Smith, whose Olympic career dated all the way back to 1972 when she ran in the 1,500 meters. In 1976 she ran the race again, and she qualified for the U.S. team in 1980, but stayed home because of the boycott. In 1988 she had finished fifth in the 10,000 meters. All this Olympic experience had earned her a place of honor as the U.S. flag bearer in the Opening Ceremonies. Now she was ready to compete in her first Olympic Marathon at the age of thirty-nine.

Though Larrieu-Smith was the oldest runner in the race, thirty-seven-year-old Lorraine Moller of New Zealand had the most experience at the marathon distance. She had won her first eight marathons, run between 1979 and 1981, and had added another seven wins to those in the decade since. The day before the Barcelona race, Moller learned of the death of her ex-husband Ron Daws. Daws had been a U.S. marathoner and had taught Moller much of what she knew about the race. "In a way," said Moller, "this race was a tribute to him."[19] Moller knew if she was ever to win an Olympic medal in the marathon, now was the time.

The team from the Commonwealth of Independent States, also known as the Unified Team, fielded some serious contenders, but perhaps their best hope was forced to stay at home. The former Soviet republics decided to choose their field based on results of the Los Angeles Marathon, and so chose a trio that included Madina Biktgirova and Valentina Yegorova. Biktgirova had been first among Unified finishers in Los Angeles in March, with a time of 2:26:23. The following month, Olga Markova ran a stunning 2:23:43 in the Boston Marathon and Unified Team officials were faced with a dilemma—stick to the rules they had set for qualifying and keep the team that had been chosen at Los Angeles, or give the boot to third-place qualifier Yegorova and replace her with Markova who was more likely to win a medal. They decided to leave the team as it was, leaving a major contender on the sidelines.

With the heat bearing down on them and the promise of a hilly climb up Montjuic at the end of the race, the runners started the Barcelona race at what world-class marathoners consider a snail's pace. Wary of the effects of the weather, they took drinks at every opportunity. The front pack was made up of some two dozen runners when Biktgirova made the first move at about twelve miles.

Biktgirova ran in the lead for a mile before her teammate Yegorova caught up with her. Yegorova ran a 5:17 mile in her effort to keep contact with the leader, a risky move in such hot weather. But the move paid off, and she soon passed her teammate and pulled into a lead of 100 yards. Officials from the Unified team might have thought to congratulate themselves for not dropping Yegorova from the team, but they knew the race was not over yet. Yegorova was running at a pace that no one could keep up for the remainder of the race.

Past twenty-one miles, she slowed, and faced the prospect of the climb up Montjuic to the Olympic Stadium. Yegorova passed the statue of Christopher Columbus, which marked the twenty-two mile mark, in the lead, but soon she could no longer hold off the challenge from behind. The challenge came from Yuko Arimori of Japan who took only a mile to close a twenty-one second gap.

As the two leaders began the climb up Montjuic, running so close that they nearly bumped each other, Lorraine Moller had pulled away from the rest of the pack and into third place. Though 200 yards behind the leaders and not able to mount a challenge to them, she appeared to have a lock on the bronze medal. Lisa Ondieki had dropped out of the race at seventeen miles. She had been forced to drink an unfamiliar replacement drink, she explained later, and it had given her stomach pains.

Though Arimori had caught up with Yegorova, her surge faded somewhat when she reached the leader, and she could not mount a charge into the lead. So, as they continued the climb up Montjuic, the two runners staged a side-by-side duel, just as the top two finishers in the men's race would do. Yegorova, however, was revitalized by Arimori's failure to take the lead. With the stadium in sight she appeared much fresher than the Japanese runner. About 200 yards outside the stadium, Yegorova made her move, breaking away from her challenger.

"It was all quite easy," she said after winning the gold in a time of 2:32:41. For her part, Arimori was thrilled to take home a silver medal—the first women's medal for Japan in track and field since 1928. Japan would take second in both the men's and women's marathons in Barcelona. Moller held on to finish in third place.

Because Yegorova had waited until just outside the stadium to make her final surge, the finish was the closest yet in Olympic Marathon competition. Yegorova won by just eight seconds, closer than any previous men's Olympic Marathon, and much closer than the previous women's finishes. The time had been the slowest ever recorded by a women's gold medalist, but the course, the weather, and the cautious early pace must be given the credit for that.

Francie Larrieu-Smith had run with the lead pack for the first half of the marathon, but she dropped back at a water stop and was unable to make up the distance. She finished thirteenth. Yegorova's teammate, Biktgirova, finished fourth but was later disqualified when a post-race drug test showed strychnine, the very drug that Thomas Hicks had used to help him to a gold medal in the 1904 marathon.

29

The Games of the XXVI Olympiad: Atlanta, 1996

In the early morning of Sunday July 28, 1996, just a day after a bomb exploded in Centennial Olympic Park, eighty-six women lined up to compete in the fourth Women's Olympic Marathon. They represented fifty-one countries, astounding proof that women's long-distance running was truly international. Among the runners returning from previous Olympics were the defending gold medalist Valentina Yegorova of Russia, 1992 silver medalist Yuko Arimori of Japan, 1992 bronze medalist and veteran of all three previous women's Olympic marathons Lorraine Moller of New Zealand, and Katrin Dörre-Heinig (formerly Katrin Dörre), who had captured bronze in Seoul in 1988. Despite the experience represented by these veterans, none was the prohibitive favorite in Atlanta.

That distinction belonged to Uta Pippig of Germany, who had won the past three Boston Marathons. Pippig's Olympic experience had come not in the marathon but in the 10,000 meters race, in which she finished seventh in Barcelona. Pippig was born in East Germany and as a youngster was taken into the East Germany sports system where coaches tried to sneak anabolic steroids into her morning vitamins until her physician parents recognized the pills and told Uta not to take them. In 1988 her trip to the Seoul Olympics was cancelled by officials because her boyfriend had questioned the government's travel policy. On January 3, 1990, three months after the fall of the Berlin wall, Pippig and her boyfriend defected, crossing the border with three suitcases and no money. With the fall of the

East German government not long after, they were among the final defectors from that country. By 1996, Pippig, like many international distance stars, was living and training in Boulder, Colorado.

Among the other favorites in the race were Manuela Machado of Portugal, who had won the marathon at the World Championships the previous year on a hot and humid day in Sweden. Most of the entrants into the Olympic race assumed that the ability to perform well in the heat would be essential to victory in Atlanta, but the morning dawned cool with a slight drizzle. While conditions were undoubtedly humid, the heat that so many of the athletes had trained for would not be a significant factor in the race.

Like the men's race, the women's marathon began at 7:05 A.M. with three laps around the track of Olympic Stadium. The women left the stadium to the cheers of a sparse crowd of early risers, but when they returned, the stadium would be packed with fans for the morning session of track and field competition. Almost as soon as the runners were out of the stadium and on the streets, Uta Pippig surged to the lead separating herself from the pack and gradually putting more and more distance between herself and other runners. Many speculated that her strategy was to establish a lead in the coolest part of the race, hoping the sun would come out in the latter stages making it impossible for the pack to reel her in. In any case, like Joan Benoit in 1984, Pippig continued to pull away from the large chase pack over the early miles.

By the five-mile point, her lead was twenty-two seconds and the chase pack consisted of fourteen runners, including most of those who had been given a chance to medal by pre-race pundits. At six miles the lead was thirty-two seconds. But just as Pippig seemed on the verge of building an insurmountable lead, her pace began to slow. Unable to build her lead in the seventh mile, she saw it trimmed back to twenty-two seconds by the end of the eighth mile. A difficult uphill in that mile had done nothing to re-energize her running. By the nine-mile mark the chase pack had been whittled down to six runners—Katrin Dörre-Heinig, Yuko Arimori, Valentina Yegorova, and Manuela Machado, all of whom were well-known runners with excellent medal chances, plus Lida Simon of Romania and Fatuma Roba of Ethiopia. Pippig still held to her lead but by ten miles it was only fifteen seconds and shrinking fast.

Many runners mentioned that the enthusiasm of the Atlanta fans propelled them through the streets during the marathon. The Japanese fans were especially in evidence, with long-distance running being one of the most popular sports in that country. Arimori saw thousands of Japanese flags waving on the sidewalks as she and the others closed in on Pippig. In some places, enthusiastic fans nearly blocked the runners' path, stepping near or even on the painted blue line that showed the shortest route through the winding streets and that often came within a foot or two of the curb. But the enthusiasm of the fans was tempered enough to prevent any serious interference and the leaders moved on toward the turnaround point.

Just past the ten-mile point, Dörre-Heinig dropped a few yards behind the chase pack, but more importantly, the pack caught Uta Pippig. Though Pippig ran with the pack briefly, she soon fell behind, apparently exhausted by her early effort. She never regained contact with the leaders and eventually dropped out of the race at about the twenty-two mile point.

Meanwhile, eleven miles into the marathon, the race had started all over. Within a short time, another woman showed a willingness to surge ahead, run alone, and try to build a lead—the same strategy that had failed to work for Pippig. This time the runner was not an Olympic veteran or world champion, but a policewoman from Addis Ababa named Fatuma Roba.

Like many Ethiopian runners, Roba was not well known on the international scene. She had run against the best runners in the world only once, at the 1995 World Championships in Sweden, where she placed nineteenth in the marathon. The Olympic race was her third marathon of 1996—she had won races in Rome and Marakesh in times of 2:30 and a personal best of 2:29. Though Ethiopia had produced no world famous women runners, its history of marathoning glory on the men's side was long and impressive, and Roba immediately brought back memories of the late Abebe Bikila and Mamo Wolde, who was still imprisoned in his homeland. Because of the secretive nature of Ethiopian training, no one could be sure just what Roba had done to prepare for this race, but whatever form her training had taken, it had been effective.

Roba, who hoped one day to be a coach and perhaps inspire other young Ethiopian women to take up running, now found herself not only leading the Olympic Marathon as the runners passed through the turnaround point, but increasing her lead with each passing mile. At fifteen miles, she led the field by twenty-two seconds, by seventeen miles that lead had increased to fifty-three seconds. She looked relaxed and smooth as she glided down Peachtree Road, smiling and waving at the occasional fans who waved Ethiopian flags at her. At one point she even reached out and stroked a flag that a fan was holding, kissing her hand where it had touched the symbol of her country.

By the eighteen-mile point Roba's lead was over a minute and the other runners began what seemed to be the battle for silver. Arimori made a break from the chase pack and that pack finally fell apart, leaving Yegorova in third place. By twenty miles, though, Yegorova had caught up with Arimori and moved into second. The same two runners who had battled for the gold in Barcelona now looked to be vying for the silver in Atlanta.

With the chase pack dissolved, Katrin Dörre-Heinig, who had fallen off the pace much earlier in the race, now climbed back into possible medal contention, moving into fourth place behind Arimori at about the twenty-three mile mark. Meanwhile, a refreshed looking Fatuma Roba skipped the final water station and headed for Olympic Stadium. There, a standing ovation greeted her as she circled the track and finished the race before the next competitor had even entered the stadium. Roba knelt and kissed the track after crossing the finish line and then began her victory lap-hardly slowing down, it seemed, from the pace she had set in the race.

As Roba jogged around the outside of the track, Valentina Yegorova ran toward the finish on the inner lanes, clinching the silver though she finished a full two minutes behind the winning time of 2:26:05. Thirty-four seconds later came Arimori, who hung on to edge Dörre-Heinig for the bronze by six seconds.

Fatuma Roba was the first African woman to win a medal in the Olympic Marathon. Yegorova and Arimori joined Rosa Mota as two-time medalists in the event. Even as the victors circled the track, dramatic finishes continued. Anne Marie Lauck finished tenth, giving the United States a tie for its second best finish ever, but she collapsed on the track after crossing the line. Medical personnel carried her off the track and treated her for dehydration and cramps and she quickly recovered. In forty-sixth place, Lorraine Moller crossed the line becoming the only woman to finish all four Olympic Marathons. Sixty-five of the eighty-six starters finished the race, but none looked as fresh and rested as Fatuma Roba—the newest member of Ethiopia's pantheon of great marathoners.

Epilogue

What sets the Olympic Marathon apart from other footraces? It is some mystical combination of those two words "Olympic" and "Marathon."

The Olympics come only once in four years. In the next century while 100 winners of the Boston, New York, and other marathons are crowned, the Olympics will crown only twenty-five. While someone who runs in Boston and has a bad day can always come back the next year and the next, many runners have only one opportunity to compete in the Olympic race. A bad day means no Olympic medal. Yet the Olympics are considered by most athletes the ultimate sporting event. They have captured the imagination of spectators as well. Little could Pierre de Coubertin imagine how the movement he created would grow and change. Though some of his ideals, such as amateurism, have been left behind, his vision of a peaceful competition that would embrace all the countries of the world and in which each athlete would be honored to compete, has nearly come into being. Although the modern Olympics now bear no resemblance to their ancient counterparts, they do maintain the underlying feel of mysticism and religion that were placed there by the tie to the ancient Games. The Olympics are a near religious experience for all the peoples of the world, and the one event that is truly Olympic, the only event on all the long program that was invented particularly for the revival of these Games, is the marathon.

The marathon has captured the imagination of people inside and outside the Olympic Games. While most casual runners used to content themselves with the dream of running a ten-kilometer road race, now everyone seems to be training for a marathon. Over 200,000 people run marathons in the United States every year. The largest race, the New York Marathon, fields nearly 30,000 runners. For most runners, the marathon is not a contest with others, but with themselves. Even world-class competitors know that the greatest battles that take place in a marathon are internal. The marathon, like the Olympic Games, was inspired by the feats of the ancients, and that link to the past gives the race a timelessness that no other event has.

Put together these two almost mystical words, "Olympic" and "Marathon," and you have a race like no other, a race that crowns as its champions those who dig deep, those who conquer themselves, those who survive. Because of its infrequency, because it is so often run in the summer heat, and perhaps because of the will of the gods, the Olympic Marathon rarely crowns a champion who has made his mark outside the Games. Consider the number of marathoners whose careers reached every height except Olympic gold—Clarence DeMar, who won seven Boston Marathons; Jim Peters, the first man to break 2:20; Derek Clayton, holder of the world record for over a decade; Bill Rodgers, who won twenty-three marathons from 1973 to 1983, but whose worst marathon finish was in the Olympics; Toshihiko Seko, for years invincible outside the Olympics; and Grete Waitz, the first lady of women's running who could only get silver at the Olympics.

Consider, too, the legends born at the Olympics, men and women who will always be remembered for the unexpected ways in which they competed in the Olympic Marathon, men and women whose names conjure up images of victory fit for the ending of a book—Spiridon Louis, Dorando Pietri, Hannes Kolehmainen, Sohn Kee Chung, Emil Zátopek, Abebe Bikila, Frank Shorter, Waldemar Cierpinski, Joan Benoit, and the newest members of this elite club, Fatuma Roba and Josia Thugwane.

Appendix: Top Finishers in the Olympic Marathon, 1896–1996

MEN

1896—Athens
(40,000 meters)

1.	Spiridon Louis	GRE	2:58:50	OR/WB**
2.	Charilaos Vasilakos	GRE	3:06:03	
–	Spiridon Belokas*	GRE	3:06:30	
3.	Gyula Kellner	HUN	3:06:35	
4.	Ioannis Vrettos	GRE	—	
5.	Demetrios Deliyannis†	GRE	—	
6.	Eleftherios Papasimeon	GRE	—	
7.	Evangelos Gerakakis	GRE	—	
8.	Stamatios Massouris	GRE	—	
9.	S. Lagondakis	GRE	—	

*Disqualified.
**Olympic Record/World Best.
  †Some sources reverse the finishing order of Deliyannis and Papasimeon.

1900—Paris
(40,260 meters)

1.	Michel Théato	FRA	2:59:45
2.	Emile Champion	FRA	3:04:17
3.	Ernst Fast	SWE	3:37:14
4.	Eugene Resse	FRA	4:00:43
5.	Arthur Newton	USA	4:04:12
6.	John Cregan	USA	—
7.	Richard Grant	USA	—
8.	Ronald MacDonald*	USA	—

*Only eight runners completed the race.

1904—St. Louis
(40,000 meters)

1.	Thomas Hicks	USA	3:28:53
2.	Albert Corey	FRA	3:34:52
3.	Arthur Newton	USA	3:47:33
4.	Felix Carvajal	CUB	—
5.	Demeter Velouis	GRE	—
6.	David Kneeland	USA	—
7.	Henry Brawley	USA	—
8.	Sidney Hatch	USA	—
9.	Lentauw	SAF	—
10.	C. D. Zahuritis	GRE	—

1906—Athens*
(41,860 meters)

1.	William Sherring	CAN	2:51:23.6
2.	John Svanberg	SWE	2:58:20.8
3.	William Frank	USA	3:00:46.8
4.	Gustaf Törnros	SWE	3:01:00.0
5.	John Alepous	GRE	3:09:25.4
6.	George Blake	AUS	3:09:35.0
7.	Constantinos Karvelas	GRE	3:15:54.0

8. André Roffi	FRA	3:17:49.8
9. Hermann Muller	GER	3:21:00
10. C. H. Natabaris	GRE	—

*Not an official Olympic Games. Sherring's time would have been an Olympic record.

1908—London
(26 miles, 385 yards)

— Dorando Pietri*	ITA	2:54:46.4	
1. John Hayes	USA	2:55:18.4	OR
2. Charles Hefferon	SAF	2:56:06.0	
3. Joseph Forshaw	USA	2:57:10.4	
4. Alton Welton	USA	2:59:44.4	
5. William Wood	CAN	3:01:44.0	
6. Frederick Simpson	CAN	3:04:28.2	
7. Harry Lawson	CAN	3:06:47.2	
8. John Svanberg	SWE	3:07:50.8	
9. Louis Tewanina	USA	3:09:15.0	
10. Kaarlo Nieminen	FIN	3:09:50.8	

*Disqualified.

1912—Stockholm
(40,200 meters)

1. Kenneth McArthur	SAF	2:36:54.8	OR
2. Christian Gitsham	SAF	2:37:52.0	
3. Gaston Strobino	USA	2:38:42.4	
4. Andrew Sockalexis	USA	2:42:07.9	
5. James Duffy	CAN	2:42:18.8	
6. Sigfrid Jacobsson	SWE	2:43:24.9	
7. John Gallagher	USA	2:44:19.4	
8. Joseph Erxleben	USA	2:45:47.4	
9. Richard Piggott	USA	2:46:40.7	
10. Joseph Forshaw	USA	2:49:49.4	

1916—Games Not Held

1920—Antwerp
(42,750 meters)

1. Johannes Kolehmainen	FIN	2:32:35.8	OR/WB
2. Jüri Lossmann	EST	2:32:48.6	
3. Valerio Arri	ITA	2:36:32.8	
4. Auguste Broos	BEL	2:39:25.8	
5. Jaako Tuomikoski	FIN	2:40:10.8	
6. Sofus Rose	DEN	2:41:18.0	
7. Joseph Organ	USA	2:41:30.8	
8. Rudolf Hansen	DEN	2:41:40.9	
9. Urho Tallgren	FIN	2:42:40.0	
10. Taavetti Kolehmainen	FIN	2:44:03.2	

1924—Paris
(26 miles, 385 yards*)

1. Albin Stenroos	FIN	2:41:22.6
2. Romeo Bertini	ITA	2:47:19.6
3. Clarence DeMar	USA	2:48:14.0
4. Lauri Halonen	FIN	2:49:47.4
5. Samuel Ferris	GBR	2:52:26.0
6. Miguel Plaza Reyes	CHI	2:52:54.0
7. Boughèra El Ouafi	FRA	2:54:19.6
8. Gustav Kinn	SWE	2:54:33.4
9. Dionisio Carreras	SPA	2:57:18.4
10. Jüri Lossmann	EST	2:57:54.6

*From this race forward, this was the standard distance.

1928—Amsterdam

1. Boughèra El Ouafi	FRA	2:32:57
2. Miguel Plaza Reyes	CHI	2:33:23
3. Martti Marttelin	FIN	2:35:02
4. Kanematsu Yamada	JPN	2:35:29
5. Joie Ray	USA	2:36:04

6. Seiichiro Tsuda	JPN	2:36:20
7. Yrjo Korkolin-Koski	FIN	2:36:40
8. Samuel Ferris	GBR	2:37:41
9. Albert Michelsen	USA	2:38:56
10. Clifford Bricker	CAN	2:39:24

1932—Los Angeles

1. Juan Carlos Zabala	ARG	2:31:36	OR
2. Samuel Ferris	GBR	2:31:55	
3. Armas Toivonen	FIN	2:32:12	
4. Duncan Wright	GBR	2:32:41	
5. Seiichiro Tsuda	JPN	2:35:42	
6. Ombai Kin*	JPN	2:37:28	
7. Albert Michelsen	USA	2:39:38	
8. Askar Heks	CZE	2:41:35	
9. Taika Gon	JPN	2:42:52	
10. Anders Hartington-Anderson	DEN	2:44:38	

*Actually Eun-Bae Kim of Korea.

1936—Berlin

1. Kitei Son*	JPN	2:29:19.2	OR
2. Ernest Harper	GBR	2:31:23.2	
3. Shoryu Nan†	JPN	2:31:42.0	
4. Erkki Tamila	FIN	2:32:45.0	
5. Vaino Muinonen	FIN	2:33:46.0	
6. Johannes Coleman	SAF	2:36:17.0	
7. Donald Robertson	GBR	2:37:06.2	
8. Henry Gibson	SAF	2:38:04.0	
9. Mauno Tarkiaimem	FIN	2:39:33	
10. Thore Enochsson	SWE	2:43:12	

*Actually Sohn Kee Chung of Korea.
†Actually Nam Sung Yong of Korea.

1940—Games Not Held

1944—Games Not Held

1948—London

1. Delfo Cabrera	ARG	2:34:51.6
2. Thomas Richards	GBR	2:35:07.6
3. Etienne Gailly	BEL	2:35:33.6
4. Johannes Coleman	SAF	2:36:06.0
5. Eusebio Guinez	ARG	2:36:36.0
6. Thomas Luyt	SAF	2:38:11.0
7. Gustav Ostling	SWE	2:38:40.6
8. John Systad	NOR	2:38:41.0
9. Alberto Sensini	ARG	2:39:30
10. Henning Larsen	DEN	2:41:22

1952—Helsinki

1. Emil Zátopek	CZE	2:23:03.2 OR
2. Reinaldo Gorno	ARG	2:25:35.0
3. Gustaf Jansson	SWE	2:26:07.0
4. Yoon-Chil Choi	KOR	2:26:36.0
5. Veikko Karvonen	FIN	2:26:41.8
6. Delfo Cabrera	ARG	2:26:42.4
7. Jozsef Dobronyi	HUN	2:28:04.8
8. Erkki Puolakka	FIN	2:29:35.0
9. Geoffrey Iden	GBR	2:30:42.0
10. Wallace Hayward	SAF	2:31:50.2

1956—Melbourne

1. Alain Mimoun O'Kacha	FRA	2:25:00
2. Franjo Mihalic	YUG	2:26:32
3. Veikko Karvonen	FIN	2:27:47
4. Lee Chang-Hoon	KOR	2:28:45
5. Yoshiaki Kawashima	JPN	2:29:19
6. Emil Zátopek	CZE	2:29:34
7. Ivan Filin	SOV	2:30:27

8. Evert Nyberg	SWE	2:31:12
9. Thomas Nilsson	SWE	2:33:33
10. Eino Oksanen	FIN	2:36:10

1960—Rome

1. Abebe Bikila	ETH	2:15:16.2 OR/WB
2. Rhadi ben Abdesselem	MOR	2:15:41.6
3. Barry Magee	NZE	2:17:18.2
4. Konstantin Vorobiev	SOV	2:19:09.6
5. Sergei Popov	SOV	2:19:18.8
6. Thyge Tögersen	DEN	2:21:03.4
7. Abebe Wakgira	ETH	2:21:10.0
8. Bakir Benaissa	MOR	2:21:22.0
9. Osvaldo Suarez	ARG	2:21:26.6
10. Franjo Skrinjar	YUG	2:21:40.2

1964—Tokyo

1. Abebe Bikila	ETH	2:12:11.2 OR/WB
2. Basil Heatley	GBR	2:16:19.2
3. Kokichi Tsuburaya	JPN	2:16:22.8
4. Brian Kilby	GBR	2:17:02.4
5. József Sütö	HUN	2:17:55.8
6. Leonard "Buddy" Edelen	USA	2:18:12.4
7. Aurele Vandendriessche	BEL	2:18:42.6
8. Kenji Kimihara	JPN	2:19:49.0
9. Ronald Clarke	AUS	2:20:26.8
10. Demissie Wolde	ETH	2:21:25.2

1968—Mexico City

1. Mamo Wolde	ETH	2:20:26.4
2. Kenji Kimihara	JPN	2:23:31.0
3. Michael Ryan	NZE	2:23:45.0
4. Ismail Akcay	TUR	2:25:18.8
5. William Adcocks	GBR	2:25:33.0

6. Merawi Gebru	ETH	2:27:16.8
7. Derek Clayton	AUS	2:27:23.8
8. Timothy Johnston	GBR	2:28:04.4
9. Akio Usami	JPN	2:28:06.2
10. Andrew Boychuk	CAN	2:28:40.2

1972—Munich

1. Frank Shorter	USA	2:12:19.8
2. Karel Lismont	BEL	2:14:31.8
3. Mamo Wolde	ETH	2:15:08.4
4. Kenneth Moore	USA	2:15:39.8
5. Kenji Kimihara	JPN	2:16:27.0
6. Ronald Hill	GBR	2:16:30.6
7. Donald Macgregor	GBR	2:16:34.4
8. Jack Foster	NZE	2:16:56.2
9. Jack Bacheler	USA	2:17:38.2
10. Lengisse Bedane	ETH	2:18:36.8

1976—Montreal

1. Waldemar Cierpinski	GDR	2:09:55.0 OR
2. Frank Shorter	USA	2:10:45.8
3. Karel Lismont	BEL	2:11:12.6
4. Donald Kardong	USA	2:11:15.8
5. Lasse Viren	FIN	2:13:10.8
6. Jerome Drayton	CAN	2:13:30.0
7. Leonid Moseyev	SOV	2:13:33.4
8. Franco Fava	ITA	2:14:24.6
9. Aleksandr Gozki	SOV	2:15:34.0
10. Henri Schoofs	BEL	2:15:52.4

1980—Moscow

1. Waldemar Cierpinski	GDR	2:11:03
2. Gerald Nijboer	HOL	2:11:20
3. Satymkul Dzumanazarov	SOV	2:11:35

4. Vladimir Kotov	SOV	2:12:05	
5. Leonid Moseyev	SOV	2:12:14	
6. Rodolfo Gomez	MEX	2:12:39	
7. Dereje Nedi	ETH	2:12:44	
8. Massimo Magnani	ITA	2:13:12	
9. Karel Lismont	BEL	2:13:27	
10. Robert de Castella	AUS	2:14:31	

1984—Los Angeles

1. Carlos Lopes	POR	2:09:21	OR
2. John Treacy	IRL	2:09:56	
3. Charles Spedding	GBR	2:09:58	
4. Takeshi Soh	JPN	2:10:55	
5. F. Robert de Castella	AUS	2:11:09	
6. Juma Ikangaa	TAN	2:11:10	
7. Joseph Nzau	KEN	2:11:28	
8. Djama Robleh	DJI	2:11:39	
9. Jerry Klernan	IRL	2:12:20	
10. Rodney Dixon	NZE	2:12:57	

1988—Seoul

1. Gelindo Bordin	ITA	2:10:32	
2. Douglas Wakiihuri	KEN	2:10:47	
3. Ahmed Saleh	DJI	2:10:59	
4. Takeyuki Nakayama	JPN	2:11:05	
5. Stephen Moneghetti	AUS	2:11:49	
6. Charles Spedding	GBR	2:12:19	
7. Juma Ikangaa	TAN	2:13:06	
8. F. Robert de Castella	AUS	2:13:07	
9. Toshihiko Seko	JPN	2:13:41	
10. Ravil Kachapov	SOV	2:13:49	

1992—Barcelona

1. Hwang Young Cho	KOR	2:13:23	

2.	Koichi Morishita	JPN	2:13:45	
3.	Stephan Freigang	GER	2:14:00	
4.	Takeyuki Nakayama	JPN	2:14:02	
5.	Salvatore Bettiol	ITA	2:14:15	
6.	Salah Kokaich	MOR	2:14:25	
7.	Jan Huruk	POL	2:14:32	
8.	Hiromi Taniguchi	JPN	2:14:32	
9.	Diego Garcia Corrales	SPA	2:14:56	
10.	Kim Jae-Yong	KOR	2:15:01	

1996—Atlanta

1.	Josia Thugwane	SAF	2:12:36	
2.	Lee Bong-Ju	KOR	2:12:39	
3.	Eric Wainaina	KEN	2:12:44	
4.	Martin Fiz	SPA	2:13:20	
5.	Richard Nerurkar	GBR	2:13:39	
6.	German Silva	MEX	2:14:29	
7.	Stephen Moneghetti	AUS	2:14:35	
8.	Benjanin Paredes	MEX	2:14:55	
9.	Danilo Goffi	ITA	2:15:08	
10.	Luis dos Santos Antonio	BRA	2:15:55	

WOMEN

1896–1980—No women's competition

1984—Los Angeles

1.	Joan Benoit	USA	2:24:52	OR
2.	Grete Waitz	NOR	2:26:18	
3.	Rosa Mota	POR	2:26:57	
4.	Ingrid Kristiansen	NOR	2:27:34	
5.	Lorraine Moller	NZE	2:28:34	
6.	Priscilla Welch	GBR	2:28:54	
7.	Lisa Martin	AUS	2:29:03	
8.	Sylvie Ruegger	CAN	2:29:09	

9. Laura Fogli	ITA	2:29:28
10. Tuila Toivonen	FIN	2:32:07

1988—Seoul

1. Rosa Mota	POR	2:25:40
2. Lisa Martin	AUS	2:25:53
3. Katrin Dörre	GDR	2:26:21
4. Tatyana Polovinskaya	SOV	2:27:05
5. Zhao Youfeng	CHN	2:27:06
6. Laura Fogli	ITA	2:27:49
7. Danièle Kaber	LUX	2:29:23
8. Maria Curatolo	ITA	2:30:14
9. Zoya Ivanova	SOV	2:30:25
10. Angela Pain	GBR	2:30:51

1992—Barcelona

1. Valentina Yegorova	UNI	2:32:41
2. Yuko Arimori	JPN	2:32:49
3. Lorraine Moller	NZE	2:33:59
4. Madina Biktagirova	UNI	2:35:39
5. Sachiko Yamashita	JPN	2:36:26
6. Katrin Dörre	GER	2:36:48
7. Mun Gyong-Ae	NKR	2:37:03
8. Manuela Machado	POR	2:38:22
9. Ramilla Burangulova	UNI	2:38:46
10. Colleen Stella De Reuck	SAF	2:39:03

1996—Atlanta

1. Fatuma Roba	ETH	2:26:05
2. Valentina Yegorova	RUS	2:28:05
3. Yuko Arimori	JPN	2:28:39
4. Katrin Dörre-Heinig	GER	2:28:45
5. Rocio Rios	SPA	2:30:50
6. Lida Simon	ROM	2:31:04

7.	Manuela Machado	POR	2:31:11
8.	Sonja Krolik	GER	2:31:16
9.	Ren Xiujuan	CHN	2:31:21
10.	Anne Marie Lauck	USA	2:31:30

Notes

1. Reed Howell, "History of the Olympic Marathon." *Physician and Sportsmedicine* 11 (Nov. 1983): 153–58.

2. All quotes attributed to Sohn Kee Chung in this chapter are from Ron Fimrite, "A Hero in His Native Land." *Sports Illustrated*, Special Olympic Preview Issue (Sept. 1988): 36–42.

3. Mike Spear, "Emil Zátopek Gives Modern-Day Runners the Truth Behind the Myth." *Runner's World*, 1982 Annual, 8–12, 89.

4. Richard Benyo, *The Masters of the Marathon*. (New York: Atheneum, 1983), p. 139.

5. All quotes attributed to Frank Shorter in this chapter are from Benyo, pp. 153–55.

6. Kenny Moore, "The End of the World." *Sports Illustrated* (4 Dec. 1995): 78–95.

7. All quotes attributed to Waldemar Cierpinski in this chapter are from Brian Chapman, "Waldemar Cierpinski: Olympic Marathon Champion Grants His First Interview to a Western Periodical Since the Games." *Runner's World* (March 1978): 68–70.

8. All quotes in this chapter are from Robert Morton, ed., *Los Angeles Times 1984 Olympic Sports Pages*. (New York: Harry N. Abrams, Inc., 1984), pp. 102–3.

9. All quotes in this chapter are from Amby Burfoot, "Golden Opportunity—Italy's Gelindo Bordin Saw His Chance, Took it and Ran into Olympic History." *Runner's World* (Dec. 1988): 39–41.

10. All quotes in this chapter are from Filip Bondy, "South Korean Pulls Away For a Grueling Surprise." *New York Times* (10 Aug. 1992): C1.

11. Roberta Gibb, "The First Woman to Run Boston." *Runner's World* (June 1978): 42.

12. "Lady With Desire to Run Crashed Marathon." *New York Times* (23 April 1967): E7.

13. "Runner's World Update." *Runner's World* (April 1980): 13.

14. Bob Wischnia, "A New Wave of Women Runners." *Runner's World* (Oct. 1980): 94–96.

15. Morton, p. 66.

16. Joan Benoit with Sally Baker, *Running Tide*. (New York: Alfred A. Knopf, 1987), pp. 192–93.

17. Bob Wischnia and Toni Reavis, "For the Record." *Runner's World* (Oct. 1988): 35.

18. Bob Wischnia, "Quick Thinking—Fast and Friendly Rosa Mota Used Cool Calculations to Win the Marathon." *Runner's World* (Dec. 1988): 44.

19. All quotes in this chapter are from Amby Burfoot, "Long Slow Distance." *Runner's World* (Nov. 1992): 85.

Selected Bibliography

"2:27:33—and Waiting." *New York Times,* 23 Oct. 1979, 22.

"2 Girls in Marathon Don't Have Lovely Leg to Stand On." *New York Times*, 20 April 1967, 55.

Benoit, Joan with Sally Baker. *Running Tide*. (New York: Alfred A. Knopf, 1987).

Benson, Lee, Doug Robinson, and Dee Benson. *Athens to Atlanta 100 Years of Glory*. (Salt Lake City: Commemorative Publications, 1993).

Benyo, Richard. *The Masters of the Marathon*. (New York: Atheneum, 1983).

Bergvall, Erik, ed. *The Official Report of the Olympic Games of Stockholm 1912*. Trans. Edward Adams-Ray. (Stockholm: Wahlström & Widstrand, 1913).

Bloom, Marc. "Gelindo Bordin—The Gentleman of Verona." *Runner's World*, Nov. 1989, 60–65.

———. "Olympic Flashback." *Runner's World*, Oct. 1991, 20; Dec. 1991, 34; Feb. 1992, 20; March 1992, 20; Aug. 1992, 36.

Bondy, Filip. "South Korean Pulls Away For a Grueling Surprise." *New York Times*, 10 Aug. 1992, C1.

Burfoot, Amby. "Olympia: Joan Benoit was the Hero of the First Women's Trials Marathon." *Runner's World*, July 1984, 89–96.

———. "Golden Opportunity—Italy's Gelindo Bordin Saw His Chance, Took it and Ran into Olympic History." *Runner's World*, Dec. 1988, 39–41.

———. "Out of Pride and Respect." *Runner's World*, Nov. 1992, 82–83.

———. "Long Slow Distance." *Runner's World*, Nov. 1992, 84–85.

Chapman, Brian. "Waldemar Cierpinski: Olympic Marathon Champion Grants His First Interview to a Western Periodical Since the Games." *Runner's World*, March 1978, 68–70.

Cimons, Marlene. "How Women Got to Run the Distance: The Olympic Marathon Breakthrough." *Ms.*, July 1981, 48–50.

Drummond, Siobhan and Elizabeth Rathburn, eds. *Grace & Glory: A Century of Women in the Olympics.* (Chicago: Triumph Books, 1996).

Dwyre, Bill. ed. *The Los Angeles Times Book of the 1984 Olympic Games.* (New York: Harry N. Abrams, Inc., 1984).

Fimrite, Ron. "A Hero in His Native Land." *Sports Illustrated*, Special Olympic Preview Issue, Sept. 1988, 36–42.

Findling, John E. and Kimberly D. Pelle, eds. *Historical Dictionary of the Modern Olympic Movement.* (Westport, CT: Greenwood Press, 1996).

"Fitting Trophies from a Pioneer Marathoner." *Sports Illustrated*, 28 May 1984, 26.

Gambaccini, Peter. "Olympic Marathons Are Likely to Produce Hot Times in Seoul Town." *Sport*, Oct. 1988, 10.

Gibb, Roberta. "The First Woman to Run Boston." *Runner's World*, June 1978, 42.

Giller, Norman. *The 1980 Olympics Handbook.* (New York: Holt, Rinehart and Winston, 1980).

———. *The Marathon: The Runners and the Race.* (Secaucus, NJ: Chartwell Books, 1983).

Greenspan, Bud. "Truths, Half-Truths and Myths of Marathon Running." *New York Times,* 26 Oct. 1980, E2.

———. "Abebe Bikila." *Sport*, Dec. 1986, 129.

———. *The Olympiad Greatest Moments.* Videocassette collection. (Dreamworks Television, 1996).

Grombach, John V. *The 1980 Olympic Guide.* (New York: Times Books, 1979).

Gynn, Roger W. H. *Guinness Book of the Marathon.* (London: Guinness Superlatives, 1984).

Hansen, Jacqueline. "History in the Making: Only in Oly." *Runner's World*, July 1984, 93, 95.

Henry, Bill. *An Approved History of the Olympic Games.* (New York: Putnam's, 1976).

Howell, Reed. "History of the Olympic Marathon." *Physician and Sportsmedicine* vol. 11, Nov. 1983, 153–58.

"I.O.C. Yields Power On Eligibility Rules." *New York Times*, 3 Oct. 1981, 24.

Irwin, T. H. "History and Chronology of the Modern Olympic Marathon." Master's Thesis, University of Oregon, 1973.

Jones, Jerene. "Women Marathoners Take to the Streets in London—One More Step on the Road to the 1984 Olympics." *People*, 18 Aug. 1980, 99.

Kessler, Judy. "When Avon Called, Kathy Switzer Gave Up the Marathon to Organize Women's Racing." *People*, 28 May 1979, 34–36.

Kristy, Davida. *Coubertin's Olympics: How the Games Began.* (Minneapolis: Lerner Publications Co., 1995).

"Lady With Desire to Run Crashed Marathon." *New York Times*, 23 April 1967, E7.

Longman, Jere. "Hot-Weather Marathon Concerns Athletes." *New York Times*, 15 Nov. 1994, B17.

———. "Start Time for the '96 Men's Marathon Is a Heated Issue." *New York Times,* 7 April 1995, B11.

———. "Doctor Wants Morning Marathon." *New York Times*, 22 Dec. 1995, B14.

Lucas, John A. "A History of the Marathon Race—490 B.C. to 1975." *Journal of Sport History*, Summer 1976, 120–138.

MacAloon, John J. *This Great Symbol: Pierre de Coubertin and the Origins of the Modern Olympic Games*. (Chicago: University of Chicago Press, 1981).

Mandell, Richard D. *The Nazi Olympics*. (New York: Macmillan, 1971).

Martin, Dave with Marty Post. "The American Marathon/Part 2." *Runner's World*, March 1980, 71–79.

Martin, David E. and Roger W. H. Gynn. *The Marathon Footrace Performers and Performances*. (Springfield, IL: Charles C. Thomas Publisher, 1979).

Montville, Leigh. "A Bridge to Long Ago." *Sports Illustrated*, 26 March 1990, 52–61.

Moore, Kenny. *Best Efforts: World Class Runners and Races*. (Garden City, N.J.: Doubleday, 1982).

———. "They Got Off on the Right Track." *Sports Illustrated*, 13 Aug. 1984, 60–81.

———. "The End of the World." *Sports Illustrated*, 4 Dec. 1995, 78–95.

Morton, Robert, ed. *Los Angeles Times 1984 Olympic Sports Pages*. (New York: Harry N. Abrams, Inc., 1984).

NBC Television. Coverage of 1996 Women's Olympic Marathon, 28 July 1996.

NBC Television. Coverage of 1996 Men's Olympic Marathon, 4 Aug. 1996.

"Olympic Marathon Run for Women Is Approved." *New York Times*, 24 Feb. 1981, C14.

"Runner's World Update." *Runner's World*, April 1980, 13; Oct. 1980, 11; Nov. 1980, 11; May 1981, 10.

Siebert, Wm. H., exec. ed. *The Lincoln Library of Sports Champions*. Fifth edition. (Frontier Press Co., 1989).

Spear, Mike. "Emil Zátopek Gives Modern-Day Runners the Truth Behind the Myth." *Runner's World*, 1982 Annual, 8–12, 89.

Stengel, Richard. "Salazar's Marathon Ordeal." *Time,* 7 May 1984, 106.

Swaddling, Judith. *The Ancient Olympic Games*. (Austin: University of Texas Press, 1984).

Temple, Cliff. "Olympic Update." *Runner's World*, Sept. 1979, 136; July 1980, 102.

Vecsey, George. "In Heat of the Day, 26 Miles Boils Down to 8 Seconds." *New York Times*, 2 Aug. 1992, VIII:4.

————. "This Time, Women Were Running South." *New York Times*, 2 Aug. 1992, VIII:4.

Wallechinsky, David. *The Complete Book of the Olympics*. 1992 edition. (Boston: Little, Brown, 1991).

Watman, Mel. *Encyclopaedia of Track and Field Athletes*. Fifth edition. (New York: St. Martin's Press, 1981).

White, Betsy. "A Novice from Ethiopia Dusts Field for Gold Medal." *The Atlanta Journal-Constitution*, 29 July 1996, 14.

Wilkinson, Jack. "South Africa's Race for the Ages." *The Atlanta Journal-Constitution*, 5 Aug. 1996, 6.

Wischnia, Bob. "A New Wave of Women Runners." *Runner's World*, Oct. 1980, 94–96.

————. "Quick Thinking—Fast and Friendly Rosa Mota Used Cool Calculations to Win the Marathon." *Runner's World*, Dec. 1988, 42–45.

————. "Form Chart: Our Look at the Top Contenders in the Men's and Women's Olympic Marathons." *Runner's World*, Aug. 1992, 76–77.

———— and Megan Othersen. "The Best of 1990." *Runner's World*, Feb. 1990, 80–83.

———— and Toni Reavis. "For the Record." *Runner's World*, Oct. 1988, 32–36.

"Women's Running." *Runner's World*, June 1978, 38, by Jackie Hansen; September 1978, 35, by Jacqueline Hansen; March 1979, 36, by Ruth Anderson; July 1979, 45, by Elaine Ivaldi-Miller.

Index

About the Author

CHARLIE LOVETT is the author of *Alice on Stage*, *Lewis Carroll's Alice*, and *Everybody's Guide to Book Collecting*. He is the editor of *The Proceedings of the Second International Lewis Carroll Conference* and a series editor of *The Complete Pamphlets of Lewis Carroll*. He started researching the Olympic Marathon in 1976 for a school project and ran his first and only marathon in 1979.